PRIVACY AND
BALANCING PU
AND PERS

PRIVACY AND THE DIGITAL STATE: BALANCING PUBLIC INFORMATION AND PERSONAL PRIVACY

by

Alan Charles Raul
Sidley Austin Brown & Wood
and
The Progress & Freedom Foundation

THE PROGRESS
& FREEDOM FOUNDATION

KLUWER ACADEMIC PUBLISHERS
Boston / Dordrecht / London

Distributors for North, Central and South America:
Kluwer Academic Publishers
101 Philip Drive
Assinippi Park
Norwell, Massachusetts 02061 USA
Telephone (781) 871-6600
Fax (781) 871-6528
E-Mail <kluwer@wkap.com>

Distributors for all other countries:
Kluwer Academic Publishers Group
Distribution Centre
Post Office Box 322
3300 AH Dordrecht, THE NETHERLANDS
Telephone 31 78 6392 392
Fax 31 78 6546 474
E-Mail <services@wkap.nl>

Electronic Services <http://www.wkap.nl>

Library of Congress Cataloging-in-Publication Data

Raul, Alan Charles.
Privacy and the digital state : balancing public information and personal privacy / by Alan Charles Raul.
p. cm.
Includes bibliographical references and index.
ISBN 0-7923-7580-7 (hbk. : alk. paper) – ISBN 0-7923-7584-X (pbk. : alk. paper)
1. Public records—Law and legislation—United States. 2 Freedom of Information—United States. 3. Privacy, Right of—United States. 4. Electronic public Records. I. Progress & Freedom Foundation (U.S.) II. Title.

KF5753 .R38 2001
342.73'0662—DC21 **2001050339**

Printed on acid-free paper.

Printed in the United States of America

Contents

Acknowledgments

Alan Charles Raul

The special help and input from the participants in the working dinner on digital state privacy at PFF's annual Internet Summit in Aspen, Colorado in August 2000, and at a follow-up meeting in connection with NASIRE's September 2000 meeting in Baltimore, Maryland, have been utterly invaluable. The state Chief Information Officer (CIO) community is the front line of privacy and access battles. Their knowledge, shared with me and my colleagues over the months since August 2000, has been essential to making this book happen. In particular, I would like to single out Aldona Valicenti, CIO of Kentucky (and current NASIRE President); Steve Kolodney, CIO of Washington; Carolyn Purcell, CIO of Texas; Wendy Rayner, CIO of New Jersey; and Moya T. Davenport Gray, Director of Hawaii's Office of Information Practices, for their enormous contributions.

Also extremely helpful at Aspen and beyond were Peter Swire, "Privacy Czar" at the Office of Management and Budget during the Clinton Administration; Jerry Berman of the Center for Democracy and Technology; Robert Wientzen of the Direct Marketing Association; Harriet Pearson, Chief Privacy Officer of IBM; and Professor Fred Cate of the Indiana University Law School.

I must especially thank my extremely knowledgeable and dedicated CyberLaw Group at Sidley Austin Brown & Wood for their prodigious research assistance and written contributions for this project. In particular, Jay T. Jorgensen has been instrumental in helping design, implement and write substantial components of the study. Joshua P. Galper, Achiezer "Jack" Guggenheim and Jonathan R. Spivey also researched and drafted significant portions of our work product. I am very grateful for the essential, substantive contributions from Jay, Josh, Jack and Jonathan. Thanks too to their families, and friends for understanding their time on the project, and in Jay's case, for taking in stride his "hardship" duty at PFF's Internet Summit 2000 in Aspen, Colorado.

The great efforts of our Research Librarian, and webmaster for CyberLaw@Sidley (www.sidley.com/cyberlaw), Sabrina Pacifici, and her colleague Carol Morrissey, have also been instrumental in finding and posting key information resources for this project (www.sidley.com/cyberlaw/features/privacydigital.asp). Randall C. Luce has done awesomely thoughtful and reliable work — as always — in proofing and cite-checking the draft. And Sharon Taylor has typed and assembled our work product with her constant professionalism and good cheer.

I would also like to thank PFF and its President Jeffrey A. Eisenach, Vice President for Research Tom Lenard and Senior Advisor Ed Behrens for their insights, guidance, and editorial input.

Many helpful comments and editorial suggestions on drafts of the manuscript were received, and much appreciated, from Bill Eggers of the Manhattan Institute, and formerly of Texas state government, Fred Cate of Indiana University, Steve Kolodney and Ro Marcus of Washington, Ed Behrens, and Arun Baheti, Director of eGovernment, Office of California Governor Gray Davis.

Finally, I have had the good fortune to be edited by Jim Harper, Editor of online think-tank Privacilla.org. Jim contributed significantly to the book's coherence and readability.

Errors and omissions are all mine as well as missteps I may have taken despite everyone's best efforts to steer me straight.

I also appreciate the very substantial support I have received for this project — and all of our Cyberlaw work — from Sidley Austin Brown & Wood, and Carter G. Phillips, my Managing Partner in Washington, D.C. Also, great wells of gratitude to my wife, Mary, for her loving understanding and relentless back-up and to our children, Caroline, William and Alexander, for their support and distraction.

Foreword

Alan Charles Raul

The devastating and reprehensible acts of terrorism committed against the United States on September 11, 2001 have greatly affected our lives, our livelihoods, and perhaps our way of living. The system of government embodied in our Constitution and Bill of Rights was designed to inhibit excessively efficient government. By imposing checks and balances against over-reaching governmental power, the Founders intended to promote the rule of laws, not men – and to protect the prerogatives of citizens over and above their rulers. No faction was to become so powerful that the rights and interests of any other groups or individuals could be easily trampled. Specifically, the Framers of our constitutional structure prohibited the government from suppressing speech, inhibiting the right of free association, preventing (peaceful) assemblies of people, conducting unreasonable searches and seizures, or acting without observing the dictates of due process and fair play.

After September 11, there is a risk that the philosophical protections of the Constitution could appear more than a trifle "academic." Indeed, our tradional notions of "fair play" will be sorely tested in the context of our compelling requirements for effective self-defense against brutal, evil killers who hate the very idea of America. Now that we witness the grave physical dangers that confront our families, friends, neighbors, and businesses, our commitment to limited government and robust individual liberties will inevitably – and understandably – be challenged. Ensuring the safety of our citizens is the highest purpose our government must serve. Indeed, the U.S. Constitution was adopted foremost "to . . . insure domestic tranquility, provide for the common defense, promote the general welfare, and secure the blessings of liberty to ourselves and our posterity." If the government did not do all it could to prevent Americans from being attacked and killed with impunity, or even failed to "insure domestic tranquility," it would not live up to the very purpose for which our government was expressly formed in 1787. In short, there are certainly times when the government must be more concerned with protecting our concrete lives, than with protecting our intangible privacies.

It is thus the subject of this book, "privacy," where the conflict among our competing interests after September 11 is likely to be sharpest. While we all wish to enjoy "the right to be let alone," no one in his or her right mind would prefer being blown up, or having other Americans face that risk, if we can prevent it by accommodating our privacy interests to our security needs.

But America must continue to be America, and our constitutional mandates must continue to be respected.

Privacy and the Digital State argues that "privacy" is inherently relative, and is always balanced alongside of other social necessities, such as other compelling rights guaranteed by the Constitution, the interest of the public in broad disclosure of and access to government records (including personal information), and the desire to foster an efficient, productive economy as well as other socially useful activities. This is by no means to minimize the value of privacy. Rather, it is simply to recognize that it is not, and never has been, an absolute imperative before which other interests inexorably fall. I hope this book provides its readers with some additional perspective on how the balance is often struck in the recurring dialectic between "open government" and "privacy of personal information." This is hardly a perfect analogy for our post-September 11 anxieties over "combating terrorism" and "invading privacy," but it may nonetheless help shed some light on how personal privacy fares when the government must necessarily favor other interests.

* * *

The Progress & Freedom Foundation (PFF) has long surveyed and analyzed the extent to which state governments are using digital technologies to lower costs and provide better services to their citizens. The benefits of "digital government" initiatives are substantial. Citizens are better able to access information and more easily conduct business with the state. Businesses are able to comply more efficiently with regulatory and filing requirements. Costly delays and errors are reduced. Eventually, the technology will begin to drive integration and rationalization of outmoded organizational structures. Because the benefits are so significant and so apparent, the pace of digitization is accelerating, with more governments moving more rapidly than ever to deploy online services and integrate back office functions.

In the process of digitizing, however, state and local governments are making more accessible information about the identity, activities, assets, and preferences of their citizens. As state governments move to integrate and make available online increasing amounts of this historical and newly-acquired information, maintaining the balance between openness and privacy is increasingly challenging.

The states' use of their citizens' data is governed by a complex set of public policy principles and constitutional, statutory, and regulatory rules. These principles and rules determine the circumstances under which different types of information must be made accessible or kept confidential. Are these rules and principles – most of which were developed in an earlier, pre-digital era – still appropriate? What general principles should state governments use to evaluate their current policies and make needed changes?

An Overview of Privacy and the Digital State

Information privacy — the ability to control information about oneself— is one of the defining concerns of the American public at the beginning of the 21st Century. The most publicized debate over privacy has concerned the collection and use of consumer information by commercial web site operators. This book focuses instead on the government's role in collecting personal information and protecting citizen privacy. *Privacy and the Digital State* addresses the proper balance between access to public records maintained by government agencies and the privacy interests of the individuals whose personal information appears in those records. Unlike the information obtained by private companies on the Internet, government agencies typically have the legal or practical power to compel individuals to supply information in exchange for driver's licenses, benefits, or permits, and during the course of real estate transactions, legal proceedings, and other processes. The ability to compel citizens to produce information, together with the government's special obligation to open its records to the public, means that the rules that apply to the private sector are not adequate or appropriate for the public sector.

While the public has communicated great sensitivity over privacy to pollsters, this may be a little incongruous in light of the rampant exhibitionism and "tell all" behavior that characterizes modern society. Nevertheless, there are indeed real privacy problems in the Internet age. Foremost among them is "identity fraud," the use of personally identifying information about an individual to commit fraud. Recent statistics show that over 500,000 people a year are victimized by this psychologically damaging and financially costly criminal activity.

Much more vigorous enforcement of existing laws is needed to fight this terrible, and growing, problem. New laws, though, are not necessarily the answer as identity fraud is already a crime at the federal level and in most states.

In general, this book suggests that adopting new and materially different public records privacy laws to address the electronic era may be problematic or even undesirable. The existing balance between access and privacy is largely sound. Almost all states have counterparts to the federal Freedom of Information Act (also called "open records" laws) and the federal Privacy Act. These laws – and the principles that inspire them – reflect society's *dual* interests in protecting public access as well as privacy. It would therefore be both constitutionally dangerous and socially unpredictable to overhaul the prevailing statutory balance just because personal information is migrating to digital formats. As Senator Christopher Dodd said in early 2001, "Legislation introduced at first blush can have deep unintended consequences."

Two U.S. Supreme Court decisions handed down at the end of the term in 2001 reflect the tensions and complexities in our attitudes and rules about privacy. In *Bartnicki v. Vopper*, for example, a divided slate of Justices concluded that the First Amendment interest in an unfettered flow of information outweighed privacy interests. In this case, a cellular telephone call was illegally intercepted and the participants' indiscreet conversation (about "blowing up" the front porches of recalcitrant school board members) was provided to the news media for public broadcasting. The Court refused to penalize the press for publicizing the private telephone call, and struck down the Electronic Communications Privacy Act's pro-privacy/anti-public disclosure provisions because of a conflict with the First Amendment. In *Kyllo v. U.S.*, where the government rather than the press was invading privacy, the Court found that the use of "sense-enhancing technology" (*i.e.*, a thermal imager) to measure heat emanating from the outside of house (where marijuana plants were being cultivated) constituted an unreasonable, and (in the absence of a search warrant) unconstitutional, search. Justice Scalia's majority opinion noted that "[i]t would be foolish to contend that the degree of privacy secured to citizens by the Fourth Amendment has been entirely unaffected by the advance of technology."

Similarly, we cannot avoid recognizing that information contained in computer data banks is vastly more accessible to the public than pieces of paper stored in dusty old file cabinets in remote county courthouses. This reality unquestionably poses new challenges for personal privacy. For better or worse, this portends the end of "practical obscurity" as an effective shield guarding our anonymity. All information, no matter how practically obscure when first placed in a dusty file cabinet, can become widely and instantaneously available to anyone with sufficient interest and access to a computer. This new reality subjects the government to the heavy burden of ensuring that truly sensitive information never enters the public domain at all.

Until recently, there has been relatively unrestricted disclosure of Social Security Numbers and other financial account numbers. These practices ought to be reviewed and reformed. As a general rule, governments should not gratuitously release bank account and other financial account numbers, health or medical treatment files, the names of children, or other personal data whose disclosure would constitute a clearly unwarranted invasion of privacy. State governments should draw the line at protecting the truly sensitive personal information within their custody, but should not restrict broad public access to information that is not so acutely personal. The benefits of public access to public records is such an important element of our constitutional democracy that it must not be cavalierly sacrificed.

By the same token, state governments should maintain a relatively non-discriminatory approach to releasing information from public records. Access to information should not generally be denied on the basis of who the requestor of the information is (*e.g.*, a commercial reseller of information rather than a journalist), or the use to which the requestor intends to put the information. These distinctions are neither fair nor tenable in a world where everyone with a computer can be a publisher, a researcher or a consumer of information. Of course, some data users — like banks and credit bureaus — are themselves subject to strict privacy laws (such as the Fair Credit Reporting Act). To the extent society benefits from allowing legitimate commercial users to obtain personal information, and those users are themselves regulated, it is reasonable and appropriate to provide certain government records to them that are not necessarily generally available to other requesters, or the general public, who are unrestrained by strict confidentiality requirements.

Access to public records versus protection for personal privacy involves inevitable tradeoffs between important social goals. Foremost among the benefits of access is promoting greater government accountability to the people. Without access to public records, fraud, waste and abuse are more difficult to detect. If governments withhold too much information on privacy grounds, the government's own activities become less transparent. On the other hand, to protect against unwarranted invasions of privacy, governments must withhold truly sensitive information and ensure that they do not collect more personally identifying information than is necessary to carry out government programs or to customize electronic government offerings for the benefit of their citizens.

While the federal government — particularly the IRS — collects prodigious quantities of personal information from members of the public, it is not nearly as varied, detailed, and commercially useful as the information collected by state, county, city, and local governments across the country.

This information helps consumers obtain credit quickly and at competitive rates, allows property ownership to be verified, and assists in determining the market value of homes based on sales activity. The U.S. enjoys a particularly high rate of home ownership, in part, because consumers can make informed decisions about property value and opportunities for financing thanks to public records.

Accelerated credit decisions are possible because of ready access to public record information about consumers. Major financial decisions in the U.S. can be made very quickly, compared to other countries. This also keeps down the cost of credit because information can be assembled routinely and efficiently from the public records, rather than being recreated for each credit decision.

Of course, journalists rely on the public record to retrieve information and uncover allegations of government wrongdoing. Law enforcement relies on the public record to fight crime. Public record information can also help track down missing family members, heirs, other beneficiaries, witnesses, tax evaders, and deadbeat parents.

While the benefits to democratic openness, government accountability and commercial efficiency are manifest, some see a dark side to easy access to electronic information. Concerns over harassment, identity fraud, and other abuses have increased as more and more information is stored electronically and made available online.

This book argues that open access to public information and sensitivity to personal privacy can, and must, be effectively balanced by all levels of government. One key to assuring sufficient protection for personal privacy is for governments to identify a limited range of specific categories of personal information that are so particularly personal and sensitive that they deserve the highest level of protection.

This book also suggests that each state governor should (a) appoint a Public Information and Privacy Task Force to evaluate and implement existing open access and privacy laws in their respective states, (b) appoint a Public Information and Privacy Officer (who could also be the State's Chief Information Officer), (c) adopt Public Information and Privacy Principles to assure that the appropriate balance between open access and privacy is achieved, and (d) authorize the appointment of Privacy Contact Officers in each unit of state government to address privacy-related complaints and questions. To the extent necessary to guarantee the privacy of acutely personal information, legislation should not be ruled out. It is more likely, however, that a combination of enlightened executive action and meaningful legislative oversight should suffice to maintain the appropriate balance without the need for substantial new statutory enactments. This is preferable because any new legislation, especially unnecessary legislation, poses unpredictable consequences and risks overturning the existing constitutional balance.

In the following pages, this book provides an introduction to privacy generally, and especially identity fraud. The leading position of federal law sets the stage for background on the nature of public records and public records privacy. Weighing the social benefits and risks of relatively open access to public records shows the crucial importance of striking a balance between privacy and access. The concluding chapter discusses "best practices" and recommendations, while appendices summarize the existing public records privacy regimes in selected states, Canada and Australia.

It bears noting that the State of Washington, which was recently awarded The Progress & Freedom Foundation's digital state award for the year 2000, has already adopted a well-balanced approach to open access and privacy protection. In Washington State, this dialectic has played itself out largely through thoughtful executive action pursuant to a comprehensive executive order issued by Governor Gary Locke and the establishment of a "Governor's Work Group on Commercial Access to Government Electronic Records." The State of Texas, under former Governor George W. Bush, has also produced a wealth of impressive e-Government and privacy summaries, analyses and thought pieces (including a paper on customization of government websites to serve citizen interests more effectively).

In the concluding chapters I offer a "model action plan," together with recommended "public information and privacy principles," for consideration by state executives, administrators, and legislators. The more salient action items and principles are noted here:

- Governments must help educate citizens to exercise their individual power – and responsibility – to protect themselves.
- State governors should establish Public Information and Privacy Task Forces and designate Public Information and Privacy Officers.
- All units of state government should designate Privacy Contact Officers to respond to privacy complaints and questions from members of the public.
- Each state should adopt Public Information and Privacy Principles.

- Personal information that would constitute an unwarranted invasion of privacy must never be placed online in a publicly accessible database.
- Open access to government records should be promoted as much as possible without harming privacy interests.
- Disclosure of personal information in the following sensitive data categories should, as a general rule, be severely restricted:
- Medical records and health information
- Tax information
- Arrest and disciplinary proceedings not resulting in convictions or adverse dispositions
- Names of children and minors
- Adoption records
- Employment records
- Social Security Numbers and other personally identifying numbers
- Similar information whose disclosure would constitute a clearly unwarranted invasion of privacy and be of no legitimate public concern
- Individuals should be provided with easy access to personal information about themselves and provided with reasonable opportunities for deletion or correction of personal information consistent with law.
- Legitimate businesses may warrant privileged access to certain public records information if society at large benefits from allowing such access to prevent, for example, credit or employment fraud or deception, and if the businesses are themselves subject to appropriate privacy constraints.
- Public employees should be made aware of their obligations to maintain confidentiality of personal information and avoid seeking or recording more personal information than is necessary.
- Electronic innovation should be encouraged and overly restrictive practices must be avoided.
- Legislative oversight and executive action should be preferred to new statutory mandates.

- Privacy principles and practices should apply to all units of state, city and county government, including the courts.

Chapter 1

Introduction to Privacy Issues

We live in an era where *information* is the coin of the realm. We are all very interested, at least in principle, in the security, accuracy, and accessibility of information about ourselves. The perception that we can control our personal information is a key factor in our sense of personal privacy. The newspapers are full of articles in which the public is telling pollsters that privacy is a source of high anxiety — indeed one of the very top concerns in this new millennium.

This anxiety is well represented by *Database Nation*, a book described by Ralph Nader as a "graphic and blistering indictment" on the privacy issue. The author, Simson Garfinkel, wrote in *Database Nation* that:

> Privacy isn't just about hiding things. It's about self-possession, autonomy, and integrity. As we move into the computerized world of the 21st Century, privacy will be one of our most important civil rights. But this right of privacy isn't the right of people to close their doors and pull down their window shades — perhaps because they want to engage in some sort of illicit or illegal activity. It's the right of people to control what details about their lives stay inside their own houses and what leaks to the outside.

Even Mr. Garfinkel recognizes, however, that computers and communication networks are not fundamentally the issue. "[T]echnology by itself doesn't violate our privacy or anything else: It's the people using this technology and the policies they carry out that create violations."[1]

Other influential commentators, like Professor Amitai Etzioni of George Washington University, believe that the so-called right to privacy, rather than being endangered, may actually be overindulged. In his book, *The Limits of*

[1] Simson Garfinkel, *Database Nation* 4-5 (2000).

Privacy, Professor Etzioni argues that the common good may suffer because the conflicting social interests in public health and safety receive short shrift due to *over-weighing* privacy concerns.[2]

While Professor Etzioni may be too sanguine about the benefits of government data collection, there is no denying that the public's actual behavior does not entirely jibe with the super-high privacy anxiety communicated to pollsters. In fact, the exhibitionist, "let it all hang out," privacy-defeating streak in modern American society cannot be ignored in policy debates over privacy. The fact is that there is a general willingness— and comfort level — to trade one's personal demographics in exchange for supermarket discounts, contest entries, "free" internet service, and the like. Some wags have said the average American would trade a piece of his (or her) DNA for a free hamburger.

In his book, *The End of Privacy*, Charles Sykes describes this anti-privacy streak in today's culture. He writes:

> Fueled by our penchant for therapy and sharing, Americans share their intimacies and dysfunctions with therapists, casual acquaintances, and national television audiences. Although the effect is numbing — does anything shock us anymore? — the pressure grows for the rest of us to join in the orgy of self-exposure least we be suspected of unhealthy repression or concealing guilty secrets. . . .
>
> . . . .
>
> . . . The truth is that as much as we deplore the erosion of privacy — and we can be quite eloquent on the subject — many of us accept the violations in the name of a wide range of equally attractive virtues and interests. . . .
>
> . . . .
>
> The political and ideological threats [to privacy] are dramatically magnified by the more general spirit of the age. We are not the first culture to revel in gossip, but our distinctive contribution is not gossip, but exhibitionism.

[2] Amitai Etzioni, *The Limits of Privacy* 4-5 (1999).

> Having perfectly sound proof walls, we have become a society that cannot shut up.[3]

America in the 21st century may be the "society that cannot shut up," and Messrs. Nader and Garfinkel are undoubtedly alarmists of the first order. Still, there is something spooky about the threat of electronic peeping toms being able to piece together what we like and where we are from information compiled in massive computer databases that are correlated with other databases and matched with location information derived from global positioning systems, cellular phone transmissions, E-Z highway passes, and a plethora of wireless devices. Yet with all of our cultural proclivities in favor of full disclosure — indeed, full exposure of almost every kind — the subject of privacy in the modern era cries out for a clear-headed sense of *perspective*. The goal of this book is to provide some of such perspective, and hopefully guidance, for treatment of privacy in connection with public records and the release of government-controlled information about individuals.

Many in Washington, D.C. today are dead-set on passing elaborate new privacy legislation. And so are legislators in every state capital around the country. They will almost certainly do more harm than good unless they focus on real problems instead of illusory ones. Senator Christopher Dodd (D-CT) put it aptly when he said "Legislation introduced at first blush can have deep unintended consequences."[4] Worse than that, the privacy legislation being considered may actually divert attention away from solving the serious privacy crime of "identity fraud," the most serious privacy-related problem today.

The legislative fascination with privacy is understandable. Polls say it is on everybody's mind and new technologies are making many people nervous. "Carnivore" lets the FBI sniff out e-mail; "cookies" and "Web bugs" help Web site operators track Internet surfing habits; information submitted online is believed to facilitate the sending of junk e-mail, or "spam"; and wireless devices are being designed to beam our locations in real time.

But the fact of the matter is that none of this is entirely new, so imposing "new" solutions on the Internet or other technologies prematurely may very well have the "deep unintended consequences" feared by Senator Dodd. For instance, the FBI has been tracking and intercepting criminals electronically for decades; acquisition and analysis of consumers' shopping and spending

[3] Charles J. Sykes, *The End of Privacy* 6-9 (1999).

[4] *Dodd Takes Privacy Caucus Chairman Position*, NATIONAL JOURNAL "TECH DAILY," Feb. 1, 2001.

preferences, habits, and patterns have long been a staple of sophisticated marketing; "direct mail" targeted to potential buyers through the post office has a very substantial track record; and location information — well, this really *is* new. But very little concrete harm has actually occurred on the Internet privacy front. Even Double-Click, the Internet "network advertiser" besieged for announcing a plan to combine customer information from online and off-line sources, was recently cleared by the Federal Trade Commission (FTC). The company never actually violated any of its privacy commitments.[5]

As to location information that is beamed out from cell phones, pagers, and other wireless devices, by all accounts of the FTC's two-day "wireless privacy" hearing in December 2000, industry is not fooling around on this. The same technology that lets cell phone companies report the location of wireless 911 calls down to within 50 meters also provides wonderful marketing temptations. But the companies recognize that they cannot avail themselves of these opportunities without getting customer buy-in or the wireless business will easily and quickly go elsewhere (not to mention that many marketing uses would violate existing laws). In other words, corporate responsibility and business incentives go hand in hand where customers have tangible privacy concerns.

A preliminary report released by Robert W. Hahn of the American Enterprise Institute in May 2001 estimated (roughly) that U.S. companies could end up spending as much as $36 billion to comply with proposed, new privacy legislation.[6]

New, complicated government privacy rules will not add much protection compared to the burdens they impose. In the healthcare area, for example, the former Clinton Administration issued a medical privacy regulation running to 1,500 typewritten pages.[7] While HHS' *magnum opus* reveals very few concrete problems to be solved by the new regulation, the agency estimates that compliance costs will reach almost two billion dollars a year, and industry estimates the costs to be much higher. Tellingly, some states (like Maine and Hawaii) have passed highly restrictive medical privacy laws only to find they had to repeal or suspend the new laws. Doctors and families were barred from obtaining information they needed or wanted about patients and relatives.

[5] Letter from Joel Winston, FTC, to Christine Varney (Jan. 22, 2001) ("Re: Double Click Inc.").

[6] Robert W. Hahn, An Assessment of the Costs of Proposed Outline Privacy Legislation 23 (May 7, 2001), *available at* http://www.actonline.org/pubs/HahnStudy.pdf.

[7] HHS regulation and information on re-opening of comments available at http://aspe.hhs.gov/admnsimp.

Similarly, in the financial services field, a veritable bevy of federal regulators have *each* adopted separate rules governing the ability of banks and other financial institutions to share relatively mundane customer information with each other for the purpose of cross-marketing. Neither business nor the public is likely to benefit much from inordinately complex solutions to deal with vague or speculative problems. Indeed, the complexity of current approaches to privacy regulation may crowd out real protections while tipping the balance against people getting legitimate information that they may value.

Information about spending and browsing patterns is not really very personal; its use may be annoying, but it is not necessarily an unreasonable invasion of privacy. In contrast, Social Security numbers, bank and credit card numbers, passwords, medical treatment files, children's names, and other similar data can be put to harmful uses. To the extent that existing federal and state laws are deficient in protecting this narrow range of highly sensitive personal information, they should be revised to provide direct and uncomplicated protection. But passing complicated new regulatory regimes that merely target online marketing practices rather than deterring genuine cyber-crimes will not solve the problem. Congress and state legislatures need to identify personal information that is truly sensitive— and protect it thoroughly. Legislators will do well to separate the myriad issues that fall under the "privacy" heading and treat each one individually. "Identity fraud," for example, is a crime that is bound up with privacy. It is the clearest actual harm and the most serious driver of public concern.

A. THE SERIOUS PROBLEM OF "IDENTITY FRAUD"

Identity fraud involves the unlawful use of another person's identifying information to commit fraud. The most common forms of identity fraud are credit card fraud, unauthorized establishment of telephone, cellular, or other utility service accounts, bank fraud, and fraudulent loans.[8] While most of the monetary harm falls on credit card issuers and businesses, consumers suffer serious anguish and damage to their credit reports through the inclusion of

[8] Betsy Broder, Assistant Director for the Division of Planning and Information of the Bureau of Consumer Protection, Fed. Trade Comm'n, Prepared Statement of the Federal Trade Commission on Identity Theft Before the Committee on Banking and Financial Services, United States House of Representatives (Sept. 13, 2000), *available at* http://www.ftc.gov/os/2000/09/idthefttest.htm.

derogatory, inaccurate information. This can result in loan denials and rejected credit card applications. Resolving these problems can involve the expenditure significant amounts of time. Some have described identity theft as "the crime of the new millennium."[9]

In May 1998, the General Accounting Office (GAO) issued a report entitled "Identity Fraud; Information on Prevalence, Cost, and Internet Impact is Limited."[10] The GAO noted that no federal agency had overall primary jurisdiction for the investigation of identity fraud, and that it is difficult to track because there is no standard definition. The scope of identity fraud can range from unauthorized use of a credit card to total adoption of a person's identity. The Secret Service reported arrests in cases considered to be directly associated with identity fraud of around 9,000 cases a year in 1995, 1996, and 1997.[11] MasterCard International, Inc. reported that dollar losses relating to identity fraud represented about 96% of its member banks' $407 million dollars in overall fraud losses during 1997.[12] While there is no universally accepted definition of identity fraud, the GAO stated that:

> identity fraud refers to the illegal use of personal identifying information — such as name, address, Social Security number (SSN), and date of birth — to commit financial fraud. Identity fraud can encompass a host of crimes, ranging from the unauthorized use of a credit card to a comprehensive take over of another person's identity and financial accounts. In short, identity theft can fraudulently use personal identifying information to take over a person's identity and open new accounts; apply for loans, credit cards, and social benefits; rent apartments and establish services with utility companies; and engage in many other types of fraudulent activities, which can result in the loss of assets or credit worthiness.[13]

In October 1998, Congress passed "The Identity Theft and Assumption Deterrence Act of 1998."[14] The Act criminalized identity fraud and focused

[9] Sean B. Hoar, Assistant U.S. Attorney, District of Oregon, *Identity Theft: The Crime of the New Millennium*, 49 COMPUTER CRIMES & INTELL. PROP. 14, 14 (2001).
[10] GAO/GGD-98-100BR.
[11] *Id.* at 3.
[12] *Id.* at 4.
[13] *Id.* at 11.
[14] 18 U.S.C. § 1028(a)(7).

on consumers as victims. It required the Federal Trade Commission (FTC) to develop a centralized complaint and consumer education service for victims of identity fraud. It also directed the FTC to establish procedures to (1) log the receipt of complaints by victims of identity fraud; (2) provide identity fraud victims with informational materials; and (3) refer complaints to appropriate entities, including the major national consumer reporting and law enforcement agencies. The FTC unveiled a new "U.S. government central website for information about identity theft," www.consumer.gov/idtheft, on January 29, 2001.

Congressman James A. Leach, while Chairman of the Committee on Banking and Financial Services of the U. S. House of Representatives, said that:

> [t]he magnitude of the identity theft threat facing consumers and financial institutions can only be described as staggering. According to statistics presented at [a September 2000] hearing, over 500,000 are victimized by identity theft each year. Victims of this crime are left not only with battered credit ratings that can take years to repair, but with the considerable psychological baggage that comes from having one's financial and personal privacy so fundamentally violated. The losses from identity theft to financial institutions – from large multinational credit issuers to small community banks – are enormous.[15]

Significantly, Congressman Leach did not attribute the rise of identity fraud to inadequate statutory protections. Rather, Congressman Leach attributed it to "insufficient law enforcement resources . . . being dedicated to identity theft crimes at the Federal, State and local levels."[16]

It is important to bear in mind the distinction between adequate statutory measures and inadequate enforcement efforts. As Congressman Leach pointed out, Congress passed the Identity Theft and Assumption Deterrence Act in 1998 and prohibited so-called "pretext calling" in the 1999 Gramm-Leach-Bliley Financial Modernization Legislation. As of September 2000, approximately 39 states had enacted laws relating to identity fraud, including 22 that had specifically criminalized it. In the FTC's testimony to the Senate

[15] Letter from James A. Leach, Chairman, House Committee on Banking and Financial Services, to Attorney General Janet Reno (Sept. 18, 2000), *available at* http://www.house.gov/banking/91800pr.htm.

[16] *Id.*

Committee on the Judiciary in March 2000, the agency noted that many states have enacted statutes specifically criminalizing identity fraud, or are considering further legislation to assist victims of identity fraud and help victims clear up their credit records.[17]

Congressman Leach expressed exasperation that law enforcement agencies have not made combating identity fraud more of a priority. The House Banking Committee held hearings to highlight a lack of meaningful enforcement efforts. The Committee found a climate of "lawlessness" exemplified by advertisements in legal trade journals and on the Internet offering bank account and other confidential information for sale, apparently in plain contravention of the Gramm-Leach-Bliley Act's anti-pretext calling provisions.

The 106th Congress also adopted the "Internet False Identification Prevention Act of 2000."[18] The new Act was intended to ensure that the Attorney General and the Secretary of the Treasury vigorously investigate and prosecute the creation and distribution of false identification documents on the Internet.

All of this legislative activity — and enforcement inactivity — is worth bearing in mind when we consider whether new statutory regimes are required to protect the privacy of sensitive information contained in public records, and also whether the burgeoning risks of identity fraud call for more aggressive and thoughtful executive action or new statutory regimes.

Most of the privacy legislation being considered in Washington and in the states will not stop or slow identity fraud. In fact, it may even divert attention — and resources — away from deterring and catching criminals. It may lull the public into believing that the true risks to personal and financial privacy are addressed through new policies aimed at restricting marketing.

Anti-crime privacy initiatives are needed. If, as Representative Joe Barton has said, "this is going to be the privacy Congress," and "privacy is . . . the civil rights issue of this decade," as Congressman Ed Markey commented recently, then legislators must provide more oversight and more dollars to guarantee that as much energy as possible is deployed in the war against identity criminals.[19]

[17] FTC, Prepared statement of the Federal Trade Commission on identity theft (Mar. 7, 2000), *available at* http://www.ftc.gov/os/2000/03/identitytheft.htm

[18] S.2924 amended 18 U.S.C § 1028.

[19] *See supra* note 4.

B. PRIVACY AND THE STATE

As suggested in the preceding discussion, the current debate over privacy covers many issues and has been heavily driven by concerns with identity fraud. It has centered around data collection by private business. The focus of this book is a little different.

This book is primarily concerned with the rules applying to state government agencies and the best policies for maintaining and releasing the personal information of citizens. It is not directly concerned with state, federal, or international efforts to regulate private parties or to investigate crimes through electronic data-gathering and surveillance.[20]

In contrast to the public sphere, the consumer in a private transaction has a complete, if sometimes difficult, choice whether or not to engage in a transaction and whether or not to reveal personal information.[21] Governments, on the other hand, can compel citizens to report information about themselves and their activities. Individuals cannot reasonably avoid many government transactions, like getting a driver's license. As Solveig Singleton of the Competitive Enterprise Institute has noted: "In the course of enforcing tax, highway, and public health regulations, the government has far more power to collect information than any private company, and more power to act on that information once it is collected."[22] The government's

[20] Examples of information-privacy matters that are collateral to this project are: (1) the state and federal wiretapping statutes, *see, e.g.* 18 U.S.C. §§ 2510-2522; (2) the Electronic Communications Privacy Act of 1986, Pub. L. No. 99-508, 100 Stat. 1848 (codified in sections of 18 U.S.C. including §§ 2510-2521, 2701-2711, 3121-3127); (3) the Standards for Privacy of Individually Identifiable Health Information promulgated under the Health Insurance Portability
Accountability Act, 64 Fed. Reg. 59,918 (Nov. 3, 1999) (codified at 45 C.F.R. pts. 160-164), *available at* http://aspe.hhs.gov/admnsimp/nprm/pvclist.htm; and (4) the Federal Bureau of Investigation's data-gathering software known as Carnivore, *see, e.g.*, ITT Research Inst., Draft Report: Independent Technical Review of the Carnivore System, *at* http://www.usdoj.gov/jmd/publications/carniv_entry.htm (last modified Nov. 21, 2000) (reporting the results of an independent review of Carnivore and its capabilities); Press Release, Electronic Privacy Info. Ctr., Carnivore Report Provides No Reassurance on Minitoring System's Potential for Abuse (Nov. 21, 2000), *available at* http://www.epic.org/privacy/carnivore/11_21_release.html (criticizing the independent review and raising concerns about Carnivore's capabilities).

[21] Solveig Singleton, Cato Institute policy analysis No. 295, *Privacy is Censorship; a skeptical view of proposals to regulate privacy in the private sector* (Jan. 22, 1998), *available at* www.cato.org/pubs/pas/pa-295.html.

[22] *Id.*

power over individuals, its special duty to serve the public interest in privacy, and its obligation to open its activities to the sunshine of scrutiny mean that a different approach must apply to public custodians of information.

The U.S. federal government has the most highly developed law on public records access and privacy. It provides a starting point for exploring existing law and practices, the public interests that are in tension, and the approaches. state governments should consider as they modernize both their governing infrastructure and their public records policies

Chapter 2

The Federal Foundation for U.S. Privacy Policy

Governments at all levels need information about individual citizens and groups to enforce the laws and to inform public policy deliberations. The U.S. federal government is certainly no exception. U.S. Supreme Court decisions, federal legislation, and federal statements of policy provide the leading foundation for public records privacy policy in the United States. Most of the federal government's privacy laws are aimed primarily at individuals, businesses, and the federal government itself — not the states. The federal privacy regime has given rise to landmark privacy developments, however, and continues to inspire privacy policies and practices in the states as well. Federal privacy law and practice begins, of course, with the Constitution. It is also grounded in a pair of public records laws — the Privacy Act and the Freedom of Information Act — and it includes sector-specific laws like the Driver's Privacy Protection Act and the Family Educational Right to Privacy Act.

Like the author and readers of this book, however, the Supreme Court has grappled repeatedly with the non-absolute nature of our interest in privacy. Competing social goals – and constitutional imperatives – push "privacy" forward or backward depending on the circumstances. In May 2001, for example, the Court struck down Congress' effort to protect the privacy of all cell phone conversations by prohibiting the publication of unlawfully intercepted telephone calls – even by "innocent" third parties like the press. Writing for a sharply divided Court in *Bartnicki v. Vopper*, Justice Stevens said the First Amendment's interest in protecting free speech on matters of public concern outweighed the privacy interests of union organizers who were conversing indiscreetly over a cell phone. The Court conceded these are important interests to be considered on *both* sides of the constitutional calculus but "some intrusions on privacy are more offensive than others."[23] According to Chief Justice Rehnquist, however, – who dissented, together

[23] *Bartnicki v. Vopper*, 121 S. Ct. 1753, 1764 (2001).

with Justices Scalia and Thomas – the majority's recognition of, and purported respect for, the right to privacy amounted to no more than "'mere words.'"[24] Even so, the overall federal framework protecting the personal privacy of citizens is not nearly so toothless as the Electronic Communications Privacy Act turned out to be in *Bartnicki v. Vopper*.

A. THE FEDERAL CONSTITUTIONAL "RIGHT" TO PRIVACY

U.S. law and public policy have long recognized that citizens have an interest in avoiding undesired public disclosure about personal matters. This *right to privacy*, as it has been called, has its roots in the common law privacy torts and has also taken hold in several states' constitutions. The federal Constitution guarantees protection against unreasonable government "searches and seizures" — a control on methods of collection — but does not address public records privacy in any express or direct way.

The U.S. Supreme Court has addressed the subject of privacy on numerous occasions. Aside from the "search and seizure" law-enforcement context, the Court has recognized two basic prongs for privacy protection. The first involves the interest of individuals in being able to make certain kinds of important decisions independent from government or other outside dominion. This is the particularly controversial *Roe v. Wade* line of privacy cases.[25]

The other involves the more straight-forward interest of individuals in avoiding disclosure of personal matters.[26] In the famous 1989 *United States Department of Justice v. Reporters Committee* case, the Justices stated that "both the common law and the literal understandings of privacy encompass the individual's control of information concerning his or her person."[27] The *Reporters Committee* case dealt with whether a criminal rap-sheet could be withheld from disclosure under one of the exemptions to the Freedom of Information Act. The Court concluded that even publicly available information could retain a private, "practically obscure" character if the data were scattered in disparate, remote locations. More recently, the Supreme Court recognized, over sharp dissents, a "recognizable privacy interest in

[2424] *Id.* at 1775 (Rehnquist, C.J., dissenting).

[25] *Roe v. Wade*, 410 U.S. 113, 151-52 (1973); *Eisenstadt v. Baird*, 405 U.S. 438, 453-54 (1972); *Griswold v. Connecticut*, 381 U.S. 479, 484 (1965) ("[v]arious [constitutional] guarantees create zones of privacy").

[26] *Whalen v. Roe*, 429 U.S. 589, 598-600 (1977).

[27] 489 U.S. 749, 763 (1989).

avoiding unwanted communication" and characterized that interest as "an aspect of the broader 'right to be let alone'" developed much earlier by Justice Brandeis in a 1928 dissenting opinion.[28]

Though the U.S. Supreme Court has not directly found a federal *constitutional* right to informational privacy, it has gotten close. In *Whalen v. Roe*, the Supreme Court rejected a privacy challenge to a New York statute that required reporting of medical prescriptions.[29] The Court recognized legitimate privacy concerns, but upheld the reporting because the state law contained significant protections against unauthorized use and disclosure. The Court recognized a duty to avoid unwarranted disclosure of private medical information and said the duty "arguably ha[d] its roots in the Constitution."[30]

In *Reporters Committee,* the Justices relied on various definitions of privacy, including a formulation of privacy as "the individual's right to control dissemination of information about himself" and as "the claim of individuals . . . to determine for themselves when, how, and to what extent information about them is communicated to others."[31] Even where information about an individual may already be publicly accessible somewhere in a remote or isolated precinct of the public domain, the Court endorsed the concept of "practical obscurity" to preserve the individual's remaining privacy interest. Practical obscurity is the idea that even publicly accessible information may be hard to collect or find, rendering it somewhat concealed or private. Practical obscurity is sorely tested in a world of computer databases where compiling information about someone in accessible and searchable formats is far easier and faster than past practices which worked off a lot of shoe leather.

Lower courts have built upon the privacy foundation suggested in these Supreme Court decisions. Courts consistently look to the "arguable" constitutional protections to address tangible privacy concerns. The U.S. Court of Appeals for the 9th Circuit said in 1999, "indiscriminate public disclosure of SSNs, especially when accompanied by names and addresses, may implicate the constitutional right to informational privacy . . . ."[32]

[28] *Hill v. Colorado*, 120 S. Ct. 2480, 2489-90 & n.24 (2000) (quoting *Olmstead v. United States*, 277 U.S. 438, 478 (1928) (Brandeis, J., dissenting).

[29] *Whalen*, 429 U.S. at 600.

[30] *Id.* at 605.

[31] *Reporters Comm.*, 489 U.S. at 764 n.16 (omission in original) (quoting Adam Carlyle Breckenridge, *The Right to Privacy* 1 (1970) and Allan Westin, *Privacy and Freedom* 7 (1967)).

[32] *Ferm v. United States Trustee* (*In re Crawford*), 194 F.3d 954, 958 (9th Cir. 1999) (internal quotation marks, footnotes, citations, parentheses, and alterations in original omitted).

The states' power to gather and manage citizens' personal information is not unrestricted by the U.S. Constitution. Courts have interpreted it to place certain restrictions on the states' ability to collect, use and disseminate personal data about individuals and their activities.[33] A number of constitutional provisions limit the actions that state officials may take in gathering information about crime both before a particular suspect is linked to an offense and after a suspect comes in contact with the police.[34] While state law enforcement efforts certainly generate public records, this book focuses on the issues of privacy and open access to information that is collected for administrative, rather than law-enforcement purposes.

In recent decades, individuals who object to state attempts to obtain or disseminate personal information about them have increasingly brought suit asserting that the state's activities violate a constitutional right to privacy.[35] In this context, individuals are not claiming a right to be free of improper police activity but are rather asserting that the individual— not the state — has authority to determine whether a particular bit of personal information will be gathered by the state, used, or divulged by the state to third parties.[36] For example, physicians and patients have filed a constitutional right-to-privacy suit against a statute that required them to file copies of certain prescriptions for use by public health authorities.[37] Similarly, right-to-privacy suits have been brought by applicants for professional licenses who have objected to providing the personal information required on the licensing form[38] and by state senators who were required to disclose their personal finances.[39] More famously, former president Richard Nixon challenged a federal law requiring him to surrender his presidential papers, arguing that the law unconstitutionally impinged on his right to personal privacy.[40]

The courts have accepted the assertion that there is a constitutional right to information privacy, but they have clarified that the right is not absolute.[41]

[33] The courts' interpretation of the constitutional provisions relating to individual privacy and the applicability of federal law to the states has changed over time. Because this study seeks to assist officials, commentators and citizens in analyzing the current debate over the states' record management, we address only the present constitutional privacy doctrines without discussing their historical development.

[34] *See, e.g., City of Indianapolis v. Edmond*, 121 S.Ct. 447 (2000); *Dickerson v. United States*, 120 S. Ct. 2326 (2000); *Miranda v. Arizona*, 384 U.S. 436 (1966).

[35] *See Whalen v. Roe*, 429 U.S. 589 (1977).

[36] *See id.* at 599-600 & n.24.

[37] *See id.* at 595-600.

[38] *See In re Martin*, 447 A.2d 1290 (N.J. 1982).

[39] *See Plante v. Gonzalez*, 575 F.2d 1119 (5th Cir. 1978).

[40] *See Nixon v. Administrator of Gen. Servs.*, 433 U.S. 425 (1977).

[41] *See Whalen*, 429 U.S. at 599-603; *Nixon*, 433 U.S. at 456-62.

Rather, the United States Supreme Court has stated that the "right" — or "interest" — is in the nature of an "individual interest in avoiding disclosure of personal matters."[42] The courts have explained that, when an individual brings suit alleging that state information-management practices violate the constitutional right to privacy, the individual's interest in non-disclosure must be weighed against the state's interest in carrying out the challenged activity.[43] Thus, the more urgent a state's need to gather and/or disclose personal information, the less likely it is that a constitutional privacy claim against the state will prevail.[44]

While courts have grappled with a constitutional "right" to privacy and the interplay between privacy and various state interests, Congress has set out statutes that govern the relationship between the public's dual interests in privacy and access to information. The federal Privacy Act of 1974[45] and the Freedom of Information Act[46] (FOIA) together form the backbone of federal policy on the dissemination of government records.

B. THE PRIVACY ACT

The Privacy Act, which was enacted long before the days of ubiquitous Internet access and the rapid digitization of public records we know today, was motivated by congressional concern over the growing "impact of computer data banks on individual privacy."[47] As the grandfather of federal privacy regulation, the Privacy Act was touted as "a landmark achievement

[42] *Whalen*, 429 U.S. at 599. *See also*, Francis S. Chlapowski, Note, *The Constitutional Protection of Informational Privacy*, 72 B.U. L. REV. 133 (1991); *Doe v. City of New York*, 15 F.3d 264, 267 (2d Cir. 1994) (collecting cases and concluding that "[t]here is . . . a recognized right to privacy in personal information.").

[43] *See Whalen*, 429 U.S. at 599-604; *Nixon*, 433 U.S. at 456-62; *Martin*, 447 A.2d at 1301-02 (explaining this balancing test and collecting cases that have applied it).

[44] *See Martin*, 447 A.2d at 1301-03. Certain types of personal information receive more weight in this balancing test than others. For example, a particular item of information is less likely to support a constitutional claim of privacy if the information is otherwise available in the public record. *See, e.g.*, *Doe v. Poritz*, 662 A.2d 367, 407 (N.J. 1995) (citing *Nilson v. Layton City*, 45 F.3d 369, 372 (10th Cir.1995) ("[A]n individual cannot expect to have a constitutionally protected privacy interest in matters that are exposed to public view.")). In contrast, information that impacts an individual's ability to enjoy peace in his or her own home is more likely to support a constitutional claim than information about a person's business or other outside-the-home pursuits. *See id.* at 408.

[45] Codified at 5 U.S.C. § 552a.

[46] Codified at 5 U.S.C. § 552.

[47] H.R. Rep. No. 93-1416, at 7 (1974), *reprinted in* SENATE & HOUSE COMMS. ON GOV'T OPERATIONS, 94TH CONG., LEGISLATIVE HISTORY OF THE PRIVACY ACT OF 1974, at 300 (1976).

in securing for each citizen . . . the right of privacy with respect to confidential information held by the Federal Government."[48]

The philosophy underlying the Privacy Act is evident from its statutory text. The Act provides first that, as a general rule, every person has a right to view the federal government's records about them and to correct any inaccuracies. Second, no federal agency "shall disclose any record which is contained in a system of records . . . except pursuant to a written request by, or with the prior written consent of, the individual to whom the record pertains."[49] Thus, the Privacy Act begins from a presumption of personal control over government-held data and vests individuals with the power to waive privacy in such data at their own discretion.

The Privacy Act does not ignore the benefits that flow from open access to government records, however. Congress has recognized that the proper policy for government-held personal information consists of a delicate balance between privacy and access. The Privacy Act therefore provides a number of tailored exceptions to its privacy protections, exceptions that balance the individual's control with the public's interest in efficient and accountable government. These exceptions provide that a federal agency may disclose personally-identifying data without the subject's consent (1) to the agency's own officers and employees who need the data to perform their duties; (2) to comply with the provisions of the Freedom of Information Act (FOIA); (3) for a routine use of the agency (agencies must notify the public of what these routine uses are); (4) to the Bureau of the Census for purposes of carrying out an official census or survey; (5) to statisticians and researchers as long as the data is provided in a form that does not identify individuals and is solely for statistical research or reporting; (6) to the National Archives and Records Administration as a record of historical value or for the Archivist of the United States to determine whether the record has such value; (7) to a U.S. jurisdiction for law enforcement purposes; (8) to the last known address of the individual who is the subject of the information if a person shows compelling circumstances affecting the health or safety of that individual; (9) to Congress; (10) to the Comptroller General for performance of the duties of the General Accounting Office; (11) pursuant to a court order; or (12) to a consumer reporting agency in accordance with other federal law.[50]

[48] SENATE & HOUSE COMMS. ON GOV'T OPERATIONS, LEGISLATIVE HISTORY OF THE PRIVACY ACT OF 1974, at v (1976).

[49] 5 U.S.C. § 552a.

[50] *See Id.* § 552a(b). The Privacy Act also allows the CIA, law enforcement agencies and others to promulgate rules exempting certain records from disclosure. *See id.* § 552a(j) & (k).

Most of the Privacy Act's exceptions relate to governmental use of personally-identifying data held by a federal agency. However, this does not indicate a congressional intent to abandon the principle of access. Mandated disclosure to comply with the provisions of FOIA is one of the Privacy Act's most significant exceptions.

C. THE FREEDOM OF INFORMATION ACT

Since its enactment in 1966, the federal FOIA has provided a broad right of access to documents in the possession of the executive branch of the federal government. The FOIA statute demonstrates a sweeping commitment to openness in government and has been relatively successful in achieving the benefits of access to public record information.[51] For example, the media has used FOIA to discover and report on numerous matters of public interest.[52] FOIA has also inspired numerous analogous state laws and given birth to many of the terms and concepts used in discussing access and privacy issues.

Recently, in passing the 1996 Electronic Freedom of Information Act (eFOIA), Congress found that FOIA provided substantial public benefits, leading to the "disclosure of waste, fraud, abuse and wrongdoing in the Federal Government." Congress also cited identification of unsafe consumer products, harmful drugs, and serious health hazards. Congress observed that "Government agencies increasingly use computers to conduct agency business and to store publicly valuable agency records and information," and that "[g]overnment agencies should use new technology to enhance public access to agency records and information."[53]

eFOIA was intended to promote the "benefit" side of open government and easy electronic access to public records. Congress did not mince words. It said: "[t]he purposes of this Act are to . . . foster democracy by ensuring public access to agency records and information."

The Privacy Act enforces this system of requirements, exceptions and exemptions through civil causes of action and criminal penalties. *See id.* § 552a(g) & (i).

[51] *See, e.g.*, *NLRB v. Robbins Tire & Rubber Co.*, 437 U.S. 214, 242 (1978) ("The basic purpose of FOIA is to ensure an informed citizenry, vital to the functioning of a democratic society, needed to check against corruption and to hold the governors accountable to the governed.").

[52] *See, e.g.*, THE FOI SERV. CTR., REPORTERS COMM. FOR FREEDOM OF THE PRESS, *Introduction*, *in* HOW TO USE THE FEDERAL FOI ACT (8th ed. 1988), available at http://www.rcfp.org/foiact/guide_a.html (listing several high-profile examples).

[53] Pub. L. No. 104-231, § 2, 110 Stat. 3048, 3048 (1996) (codified at 5 U.S.C. § 552 note).

FOIA's expansive right of access counterbalances the Privacy Act's restrictions on access to government data.[54] At the same time, however, FOIA has its own list of nine exemptions that address the need for privacy.[55] This structure makes clear that Congress' foundational premise in enacting FOIA was to find a middle ground — a way to balance the public's interest in both access to public records and in personal privacy.[56] As such, FOIA provides a good example for states that are struggling with proposals to drastically open or unduly restrict public access to information in their electronic records.

The process for obtaining government documents under FOIA begins with a written request directed to the relevant federal agency. An agency that receives such a request must make the requested records "promptly available" for inspection unless a requested record falls within one the nine specified exemptions. These exemptions cover records that are (1) properly classified for purposes of national defense or foreign policy under criteria set forth in an executive order; (2) "related solely to the internal personnel rules and practices of an agency"; (3) specifically exempted from FOIA by statute (leaving no discretion regarding disclosure); (4) privileged or confidential trade secrets or financial information; (5) inter- or intra-agency memoranda or letters that would not otherwise be available to the public by law; (6) "personnel and medical files and similar files the disclosure of which would constitute a clearly unwarranted invasion of personal privacy"; (7) certain records compiled for law enforcement purposes, including those that "could

[54] *See* 5 U.S.C. § 552a(b)(2) (providing an exception from the Privacy Act for compliance with FOIA).

[55] *See id.* § 522(b)(1)-(9).

[56] FOIA's legislative history confirms that this was Congress' purpose. *See, e.g.*, S. Rep. No. 89-813, at 3 (1965) ("At the same time that a broad philosophy of 'freedom of information' is enacted into law, it is necessary to protect certain equally important rights of privacy with respect to certain information in Government files, such as medical and personnel records.... It is not an easy task to balance the opposing interests, but it is not an impossible one either. It is not necessary to conclude that to protect one of the interests, the other must, of necessity, either be abrogated or substantially subordinated. Success lies in providing a workable formula which encompasses, balances, and protects all interests, yet places emphasis on the fullest responsible disclosure."); H.R. Rep. No. 89-1497, at 6 (1966) ("It is vital to our way of life to reach a workable balance between the right of the public to know and the need of the Government to keep information in confidence to the extent necessary without permitting indiscriminate secrecy. The right of the individual to be able to find out how his Government is operating can be just as important to him as his right to privacy and his right to confide in his Government. This bill strikes a balance considering all these interests."). *See also* Paul A. Rubin, Note, *Applying the Freedom of Information Act's Privacy Exemption to Requests for Lists of Names and Addresses*, 58 FORDHAM L. REV. 1033, 1033 (1990) ("The Freedom of Information Act ... recognizes both the value of providing public access to government information and the need to protect the privacy of individual citizens.").

reasonably be expected to constitute an unwarranted invasion of personal privacy"; (8) reports on the condition of financial institutions produced by, on behalf of, or for the use of an agency that regulates such institutions; and (9) geological and geophysical information concerning wells.[57]

There are several principles that can be drawn from these exemptions. First, it is apparent that Congress was concerned about the potential for FOIA requests to be used to obtain an unfair competitive advantage. Second, Congress tried to craft the FOIA exemptions to prevent harm to the public—whether the risk of that harm stems from criminals or investors who would trade on confidential information regarding a company or bank. Finally, Congress thought that certain files held by the federal government contain information personal enough in nature that its disclosure was especially likely to constitute an "unwarranted invasion of personal privacy."[58]

Notably, even though Congress determined that privacy interests would sometimes outweigh the need for access, it also recognized that not all records that fall within a FOIA exemption would raise privacy concerns sufficient to outweigh access. Accordingly, when requested records are covered by one of FOIA's statutory exemptions, the agency may withhold the records, but it is generally not required to do so. Additionally, if an agency determines that a record should be withheld under one of the FOIA exemptions, it must provide the requesting person with "[a]ny reasonably segregable portion of" the record.[59] This is a disclosure-oriented framework. Consistent with it, former President Clinton and Attorney General Reno instructed federal agencies and department heads not to withhold information that technically falls within one of the permissive FOIA exemptions unless withholding the record is necessary to prevent foreseeable harm to an interest that is protected by an exemption.[60]

The Privacy Act and FOIA are general public record laws that mostly affect the federal government itself. Other federal laws govern specific categories of public records in the hands of states. These include the

[57] *See* 5 U.S.C. § 522(b).

[58] *Id.* § 522(b)(6) & (7)(C). These principles provide a useful starting point for analyzing state efforts to balance open access in state records with privacy interests.

[59] *Id.* § 552(b).

[60] *See* FOIA Update, Attorney General Reiterates FOIA Policy (Spring 1997), *available at* http://www.usdoj.gov/oip/foia_updates/Vol_XVIII_2/page1.htm ("'[A]n agency should make a discretionary disclosure of exempt information whenever it is possible to do so without foreseeable harm to any interest that is protected by a FOIA exemption; an agency should withhold information under the FOIA only when it is necessary to do so. . . .'" (omission in original) (quoting a Department of Justice memorandum reiterating the Attorney General's instructions on the implementation of FOIA.)).

Driver's Privacy Protection Act and the Family Educational Right to Privacy Act.

D. THE DRIVERS PRIVACY PROTECTION ACT

The Drivers Privacy Protection Act[61] (DPPA) regulates the disclosure and resale of personal information contained in state driver's license records (DMV records). Enacted in 1994, the DPPA responded to congressional concern that citizens have little choice but to provide the information necessary to register a vehicle or obtain a driver's license, yet they are often not provided with an opportunity to restrict the disclosure and sale of that information.[62]

To address this problem, the DPPA prohibits the states or their officers from "knowingly disclos[ing] or otherwise mak[ing] available to any person or entity personal information about any individual obtained by [a motor vehicle] department in connection with a motor vehicle record."[63] The DPPA defines a "motor vehicle record" as "any record that pertains to a motor vehicle operator's permit, motor vehicle title, motor vehicle registration, or identification card issued by a department of motor vehicles." "Personal information" is data "that identifies an individual, including an individual's photograph, Social Security number, driver identification number, name, address (but not the 5- digit zip code), telephone number, and medical or disability information."[64]

These broad definitions bring a vast amount of the states' data within the DPPA's coverage, but that does not mean that Congress totally rejected the idea that the public should have some level of access to DMV records. Rather than rejecting the principle of open access outright, Congress crafted the DPPA (like FOIA) to cast a balance between access and privacy. For example, the DPPA's prohibition on the disclosure of personal information does not apply if the person who is the subject of the information consents to the release of their data. At first Congress tailored this consent exception as an opt-out procedure: states could divulge drivers' personal data as long as they provided an opportunity for drivers to block such disclosure.[65] However, Congress recently changed that system to an opt-in procedure

[61] Codified as amended at 18 U.S.C. §§ 2721-2725.

[62] *See generally Reno v. Condon*, 528 U.S. 141, 143-44 (2000).

[63] 18 U.S.C. § 2721(a).

[64] *Id.* § 2725(1) & (3).

[65] *See id.* § 2721(b)(11), (13) and (d) (1994 ed. and Supp. III).

whereby a state must obtain a driver's affirmative consent before disclosing the drivers' personal information.[66]

Additionally, Congress created a long list of both mandatory and permissive exceptions to the DPPA's ban on the nonconsensual disclosure of drivers' personal data. These exceptions require states to disclose DMV records "for use in connection with matters of motor vehicle or driver safety and theft, motor vehicle emissions, motor vehicle product alterations, recalls, or advisories, performance monitoring of motor vehicles and dealers by motor vehicle manufacturers, and removal of non-owner records from the original owner records of motor vehicle manufacturers to carry out the purposes of" several federal statutes. The DPPA permits states to divulge drivers' personal information for more than fourteen governmental, commercial, and private uses:[67]

> (1) For use by any government agency, including any court or law enforcement agency, in carrying out its functions, or any private person or entity acting on behalf of a Federal, State, or local agency in carrying out its functions.
>
> (2) For use in connection with matters of motor vehicle or driver safety and theft; motor vehicle emissions; motor vehicle product alterations, recalls, or advisories; performance monitoring of motor vehicles, motor vehicle parts and dealers; motor vehicle market research activities, including survey research; and removal of non-owner records from the original owner records of motor vehicle manufacturers.
>
> (3) For use in the normal course of business by a legitimate business or its agents, employees, or contractors, but only –
>
> (A) to verify the accuracy of personal information submitted by the individual to the business or its agents, employees, or contractors; and
>
> (B) if such information as so submitted is not correct or is no longer correct, to obtain the

[66] *See* Pub. L. No. 106-69, §§ 350(c), (d) and (e), 113 Stat. 986, 1025 (1999).
[67] *See* 18 U.S.C. § 2721(b).

correct information, but only for the purposes of preventing fraud by, pursuing legal remedies against, or recovering on a debt or security interest against, the individual.

(4) For use in connection with any civil, criminal, administrative, or arbitral proceeding in any Federal, State, or local court or agency or before any self-regulatory body, including the service of process, investigation in anticipation of litigation, and the execution or enforcement of judgments and orders, or pursuant to an order of a Federal, State, or local court.

(5) For use in research activities, and for use in producing statistical reports, so long as the personal information is not published, redisclosed, or used to contact individuals.

(6) For use by any insurer or insurance support organization, or by a self-insured entity, or its agents, employees, or contractors, in connection with claims, investigation activities, antifraud activities, rating or underwriting.

(7) For use in providing notice to the owners of towed or impounded vehicles.

(8) For use by any licensed private investigative agency or licensed security service for any purpose permitted under this subsection.

(9) For use by an employer or its agent or insurer to obtain or verify information relating to a holder of a commercial driver's license that is required under chapter 313 of title 49.

(10) For use in connection with the operation of private toll transportation facilities.

(11) For any other use in response to requests for individual motor vehicle records if the State has obtained the express consent of the person to whom such personal information pertains.

> (12) For bulk distribution for surveys, marketing or solicitations if the State has obtained the express consent of the person to whom such personal information pertains.
>
> (13) For use by any requester, if the requester demonstrates it has obtained the written consent of the individual to whom the information pertains.
>
> (14) For any other use specifically authorized under the law of the State that holds the record, if such use is related to the operation of a motor vehicle or public safety.

Because the DPPA directly regulates the states and requires state officers to perform certain acts and refrain from others, the state of South Carolina challenged the law as an unconstitutional infringement on the states' authority. The U.S. Supreme Court recently rejected that challenge, concluding that the regulation of DMV information is within the scope of Congress' power because of the interstate, commercial nature of both the items that the state DMVs regulate (automobiles and drivers) and the personal information itself. The Supreme Court also concluded that the DPPA's federal regulation of state databases is not an unconstitutional attempt to force the states to use their own sovereign power to regulate their citizens.[68] Given these conclusions, almost any information that states gather about their citizens may be subjected to federal regulation if the states have historically sold that information in the marketplace.

E. THE FAMILY EDUCATIONAL RIGHT TO PRIVACY ACT

Because most (if not all) state primary, secondary, and post-secondary educational systems receive federal money, the Family Educational Right to Privacy Act[69] (FERPA) is also relevant to the states' record-disclosure policies. FERPA imposes a set of record-disclosure requirements and limitations on any educational institution or state educational agency that receives federal funding.[70]

[68] *See Condon*, 528 U.S. at 147-51.
[69] Codified at 20 U.S.C. § 1232g.
[70] *See id.* § 1232g(a)(1)(A) and (B).

FERPA serves two purposes. First, FERPA requires schools and educational agencies who receive federal funding to give parents of a student (or the student themselves if they are over 18 or enrolled in a post-secondary institution) an opportunity to review the student's educational records and to request a hearing if those records are inaccurate.[71] Subject to several narrow exceptions, the educational records subject to disclosure include all items used to determine the student's educational placement and advancement.[72]

On the privacy side, FERPA generally prohibits schools from disclosing information from a student's educational records to third parties without the written consent of the student's parents (or the consent of the student if the student is in college or over the age of majority).[73] FERPA makes an exception for the disclosure of "directory information," which it defines as "the student's name, address, telephone listing, date and place of birth, major field of study, participation in officially recognized activities and sports, weight and height of members of athletic teams, dates of attendance, degrees and awards received, and the most recent previous educational agency or institution attended by the student."[74] FERPA also exempts disclosures to certain persons, officials, and organizations for specified purposes such as school transfers, law enforcement, and emergency management.[75]

FERPA and the DPPA are examples of sector-specific laws that combine with general laws like the Privacy Act and FOIA, and with U.S. Supreme Court cases, to make up the federal framework governing public records privacy and access. Only rarely does federal law directly control what states may do. More often, it provides an example that states may follow when addressing their own public records practices. Because states hold different records with different categories of information, and because they do different things with them, each must assess public records policy for itself. Each state should consider the mix of privacy and access it provides its citizens based on considerations addressed in the next chapter.

[71] *See id.* § 1232g(a) and (d); *Student Press Law Ctr. v. Alexander*, 778 F. Supp. 1227, 1228 (D.D.C. 1991). Although FERPA does not expressly provide a cause of action against the school or its sponsoring institution (which in many cases is the state), numerous courts have held that students may bring a FERPA suit against their school under 42 U.S.C. § 1983. *See, e.g. Tarka v. Cunningham*, 917 F.2d 890, 891 (5th Cir. 1990) (citing *Fay v. South Colonie Century Sch. Dist.*, 802 F.2d 21, 33 (2d Cir. 1986)); *Belanger v. Nashua, N.H., Sch. Dist.*, 856 F. Supp. 40, 46-48 (D.N.H. 1994).

[72] *See* 20 U.S.C. § 1232g(a); 34 C.F.R. § 99.3; *Belanger*, 856 F. Supp. at 48-51.

[73] *See* 20 U.S.C. § 1232g(b) and (d).

[74] *See id.* § 1232g(a)(5).

[75] *See id.* § 1232g(b).

F. HEALTH INSURANCE PORTABILITY AND ACCOUNTABILITY ACT

In 1996, Congress addressed medical privacy standards by The Act provided that the Administration must issue new regulatory standards if Congress failed to enact a further medical privacy statute within protecting Insurance

Accountability Act of 1996 (HIPPA). three years of HIPAA's enactment. After three years passed without action from Congress, the Clinton Administration issued, and the the Bush Administration subsequently endorsed, minimum federal regulatory standards to protect the collection, maintenance and exchange of individually identifiable health information.[76]

Under HIPAA's privacy regulations, covered entities must designate a privacy official; train employees on privacy obligations; obtain necessary consents for use and disclosure of information; provide privacy notices; and allow individuals to inspect personal information collected about them, and safeguard the security of such information. The regulations became effective April 14, 2001, and complete compliance is required by April 14, 2003.

[76] Pub. L. No. 104-191, § 264, 110 Stat. 1936, 2033-34 (1996); 45 C.F.R. pts. 160 & 162.

Chapter 3

Public Records Privacy

Public records privacy has become one of the key issues for the effective deployment of electronic government in Washington, D.C. and state capitals throughout the nation. A number of guiding principles caution restraint in changing the privacy landscape too dramatically or too quickly. Neither legislators nor opinion leaders should plunge ahead to propose radical overhauls of the existing balance between the public's interest in open access to government records and the public's simultaneous interest in protecting personal information. Outside of the identity fraud problem — which is significant — there does not appear to be a compelling factual case for overturning the careful, existing balance between state privacy statutes and open records acts. Thoughtful executive action and legislative oversight may be more appropriate to address privacy in the digital state than turning to substantial statutory overhauls.

Generally speaking, any information maintained by or for government agencies is a public record. The Center for Democracy and Technology (CDT) has published an excellent paper on privacy and public records setting forth an extensive sampler of public records.[77] Examples of records include:

- Driver's Licenses
- Driving Records
- Motor Vehicle Registration & Titles
- Land Titles
- Property Tax Records
- Voting Registration Records
- Occupational Licenses
- Use Licenses (e.g., ham radio, CB radio)
- Firearms Permits

[77] Robert Gellman, Ctr. for Democracy & Tech., Public Records: Access, Privacy and Public Policy (May 16, 1995), *available at* www.cdt.org/privacy/peubrecs/pubrec.html.

- Court Records
- Bankruptcy filings
- Civil Actions
- Criminal Histories
- Divorces
- Docket Information
- Juror Information
- Wills
- Law Enforcement Records
- Police Blotters
- Jail Lists
- Compiled Criminal History Records
- Political Contributions
- Securities & Exchange Commission Filings
- Financial Disclosure (Ethics) Filings
- Hunting & Fishing Licenses
- Boat, Aircraft & Other Vehicle Titles
- U.S. Postal Service Address Records

CDT notes that, while the types of records held by different jurisdictions vary, the information in public records about a given individual (and a likely source of the information) can include:

- Name and address (driver's license)
- Home ownership (land title)
- Home loan (land title)
- Assessed value of home (property tax)
- Size of home, price, physical description (land)
- Parents (vital statistics)
- Social Security number (driver's license)
- Height and weight (driver's license)
- Sex (drivers license; vital statistics)
- Date of birth (driver's license; vital statistics)
- Vision correction (driver's license)
- Selected medical conditions (driver's license)
- Selected occupations (occupational licenses)
- Make and model of automobile owned (motor vehicle)
- Automobile loans (motor vehicle)
- Driving record (driver's license)

- Political party registration (voter registration)
- Voting frequency (voter registration)
- Political contributions (Federal Election Commission)
- Selected hobbies (hunting/fishing licenses)
- Boat/Airplane ownership (license)

Categories of personal information maintained by government agencies that are not routinely available to the public include:

- Census records
- Income tax records
- Wage and personal property tax records
- Health records
- School records (except directory information)
- Juvenile criminal proceedings
- Adoption records
- Welfare and social service records
- Benefit records (e.g., food stamps)
- Library borrowing records

Having captured the types of records that comprise public records and the categories of personal information that can be found in them, we may turn to the benefits and costs or concerns with public records access. Reviewing them carefully helps set the stage for public records policy in the digital age.

A. BENEFITS OF ACCESS TO PUBLIC RECORDS

There is widespread and longstanding acceptance of the idea that the public should have access to state records. Indeed, many legislatures, state officials, and commentators have expressed the belief that public access to official records is an essential component of a representative form of government.[78] But that is only the beginning of the list of benefits accruing from access to public records.

[78] The statement of public policy in Texas' Open Records Act is illustrative. *See* TEX. GOV'T CODE § 552.001(a), *available at* http://www.adminlaw.org/ora.htm ("Under the fundamental philosophy of the American constitutional form of representative government that adheres to the principle that government is the servant and not the master of the people, it is the policy of this state that each person is entitled, unless otherwise expressly provided by law, at all times

Professor Fred H. Cate and Iowa CIO Richard J. Varn noted in their insightful paper, *The Public Record: Information Privacy and Access*:

> Our entire system of real property ownership and nearly all real estate transactions have long depended on public records. These records are used to confirm that the property exists, its location, and its defined boundaries. Buyers, lenders, title insurers, and others use these records to verify the title owner. Mortgages, many legal judgments, and other claims against real property cannot be collected without reference to public records.
>
> . . . .
>
> In sum, the American open public record allows citizens to oversee their government, facilitates a vibrant economy, improves efficiency, reduces costs, creates jobs, and provides valuable products and services that people want. As the Federal Reserve Board reported to Congress in the context of financial information: "[I]t is the freedom to speak, supported by the availability of information and the free-flow of data, that is the cornerstone of a democratic society and market economy."[79]

A report produced in Texas, *Privacy Issues Involved in Electronic Government*, also notes the practical usefulness of public records:

> Texans' home, employment, financial, and medical information held by Texas State government is open for any individual, organization, or company to acquire. Having such data open to the public is useful in conducting normal every day financial and social transactions. Legitimate

to complete information about the affairs of government and the official acts of public officials and employees. The people, in delegating authority, do not give their public servants the right to decide what is good for the people to know and what is not good for them to know. The people insist on remaining informed so they may retain control over the instruments they have created.").

[79] Fred H. Cate & Richard J. Varn, *The Public Record: Information Privacy and Access – A New Framework for Finding the Balance* 12-13 (Coalition for Sensible Public Records 1999), *available at* http://www.scpra.org.

> businesses need data from state government to corroborate information given to them by customers and to comply with government regulations. Law enforcement relies on public record information to prevent, detect, and solve crimes. Private citizens use public records to locate missing family members and heirs to estates. Researchers also use open public records to conduct studies concerning public safety, public health, crime, and an array of other subjects. Lastly, commercial users and resellers of public records often update them, correct inaccuracies and sell a revised version back to the government. They also lessen the volume of inquires that could potentially overwhelm government agencies by providing other outlets of public records access.[80]

Both reports acknowledge information privacy concerns as well.

Because public support for access to state records is so pervasive, every state has adopted some version of an open-records or freedom-of-information act that gives citizens an enforceable right to inspect an array of state records on request.[81] As discussed below, Florida has gone even further — enacting both an open records statute and making access to public records a constitutional right.[82] To ensure that the open access laws are not frustrated, state legislatures have frequently instructed the courts to interpret these laws expansively so that citizens will have wide-ranging access to state records.[83] State courts have been generally enthusiastic in following such mandates.[84] As this striking public commitment to freedom of information suggests, citizens derive many tangible benefits from open access to their state's records.

[80] TEX. DEP'T OF INFO. RES., *Privacy in Texas*, *in* PRIVACY ISSUES INVOLVED IN THE ELECTRONIC GOVERNMENT (Aug. 2000), *available at* http://www.dir.state.tx.us/egov/report/privacy.html.

[81] *See, e.g.*, Freedom of Info. Ctr., *at* http://web.missouri.edu/~foiwww/citelist.html (last modified Dec. 1, 1999) (providing citations and/or hyperlinks to the open-access or freedom-of-information laws for every state and the District of Columbia).

[82] *See id.* (providing hyperlinks to FLA. STAT. ch. 119.01-.15 & 119.19 (1998) and FLA. CONST. art. I, § 24).

[83] *See, e.g.*, Texas Open Records Act, TEX. GOV'T CODE § 552.001(a) & (b), *available at* http://www.adminlaw.org/ora.htm).

[84] For an excellent example of how courts have embraced this legislative requirement, see *Bryant v. Weiss*, 983 S.W.2d 902 (Ark. 1998), *available at* http://courts.state.ar.us/opinions/1998b/981221/98-564.html).

1. Government Accountability

The first and likely most important benefit of open access to state records is that it facilitates representative government. If citizens are to monitor and hold accountable their representatives, they need access to the data that informs government decision-making and the records of what decisions the government has made.[85]

Although open access is necessary for government accountability, there is room for personal privacy in the management of state records even under the broadest conception of government accountability. Citizens have a valid argument that they cannot fully monitor their state government's activities unless they know what information the state gathers about its citizens and for what purposes. But this process of informing citizens and holding the state accountable can usually be equally effective if the public knows what *categories* of information the state is gathering, how it is obtaining and managing that information, and to what use the information is put. For example, it is important for the public to know if the state is keeping a database of citizens' drug prescriptions, but citizen control of government is usually not meaningfully served by having the state inform curious citizens what drugs all of their friends and neighbors are taking.

2. Helping the Press Report on the Government

Closely related to the concept of government accountability is the need for journalistic access to state records. Because individual citizens lack the time, resources, and often the expertise to closely monitor the state's activities, the press has long performed a valuable public watchdog role.[86] While the press

[85] *See, e.g.*, TEX. GOV'T CODE § 552.001(a), *available at* http://www.adminlaw.org/ora.htm (expressing the Texas legislature's view that open access to state records is the people's right in a representative democracy). The idea that the public should be informed of government activities has deep roots in American history. Abraham Lincoln is quoted as saying "Let the people know the facts, and the country will be safe." George A. Krimsky, The Role of the Media in a Democracy, *at* http://www.usinfo.org/media/press/essay3.htm (last modified June 24, 1997).

[86] *See, e.g.*, http://freedomforum.org (reporting on numerous current issues and events relating to the media's government-watchdog role); Krimsky, *supra* note 85 (quoting Thomas Jefferson's statement "If it were left to me to decide whether we should have a government without newspapers or newspapers without a government, I should not hesitate a moment to prefer the latter.").

has occasionally been able to inform the public of government activities by obtaining government records outside of the normal document-disclosure process,[87] the legal right and presumptions in favor of disclosing public records facilitate the media's efforts to discover and report on government activities.[88]

Information specific to individuals may be required to maximize this benefit. A state's personally-identifying records can act as a type of super phone book — identifying those citizens who are involved with or impacted by specific issues and providing the information necessary to contact them.[89] Of course, journalists are not the only people interested in keeping abreast of issues relating to state government. Special interest groups, academics and individual citizens, among others, may also find that access to the state's information about other citizens facilitates their efforts to select, persuade, and hold accountable their state's leaders.[90]

[87] One high-profile example is the decision by the *New York Times* and *Washington Post* to publish the Pentagon Papers, which a government employee unlawfully delivered to the media for the purpose of informing the public about the federal government's activities in Vietnam. *See, e.g., New York Times Co.* v. *United States*, 403 U.S. 713 (1971), *available at* http://caselaw.lp.findlaw.com/scripts/getcase.pl?navby=case&court=us&vol=403&invol=713#714).

[88] *See, e.g.*, Dr. Peter Eigen, The media and the fight against corruption, Address at the CELAP Conference (July 8, 1999), *at* http://www.transparancy.de/documents/speeches/pe_puerto-rico.html (noting that the countries that Transparency International considers to have the lowest occurrence of official corruption often have the most far-reaching freedom-of-information laws and arguing that the public availability of government records helps the media and public oversee government activities); FOI SERV. CTR., *supra* note 52 (noting several instances where investigative reporting has been furthered by access to governmental documents).

[89] *See* Brief Amici Curiae of the Reporters Committee for Freedom of the Press, the American Society of Newspaper Editors and the Society of Professional Journalists, *Reno v. Condon*, 528 U.S. 141, No. 98-1464, 1999 WL 688443, at *1- *2 (U.S. 2000) ("Journalists depend on the First Amendment, state open records law, and the federal Freedom of Information Act . . . to obtain information from and about government agencies. The media in turn provide the public with information that allows public participation in self-government. Journalists also depend on primary source material contained in government databases, such as names, addresses, and telephone numbers, as an indispensable resource for investigative reporting.").

[90] *See, e.g.* Fred H. Cate, *Privacy in the Information Age* 28 (1997) (noting that a broad conceptualization of privacy makes it more difficult for individuals to learn the truth and thereby "facilitates the dissemination of false information").

3. Ease of Identification and Communication

As Professor Etzioni might argue, public records can provide communitarian benefits other than holding the government accountable. For example, the press, community groups, family members and others can use public records to identify those who live in a certain area, for example, or who are involved in certain activities or lines of business. State records can link individuals to specific information (such as genealogical records, financial needs, hobbies, and business interests) and provide interested parties with the information necessary to make valuable contacts. Because the states' electronic databases often contain not only individuals' names, addresses, and phone numbers, but also information about those individuals' histories, attributes, activities, and interests, the databases can be enormously helpful to a range of private parties — from individuals seeking lost friends and relatives, to credit reporting bureaus, to businesses searching for prospective customers.

Public record information can also help track down missing family members, heirs, other beneficiaries, witnesses, tax evaders, and deadbeat parents. The Association for Children for Enforcement of Support reports that public record information provided through commercial vendors helped locate over 75 percent of the "'deadbeat parents'" they sought.[91]

4. Economic Efficiencies

There are also a variety of economic efficiencies associated with access to state records. For example, even when state records were maintained primarily in hard-copy format, insurance companies, credit bureaus and, direct-marketing organizations (among others) used the states' records to obtain a large volume of information that otherwise may not have been cost-effectively available.[92]

[91] Cate & Varn, *supra* note 79.

[92] *See Reno v. Condon*, 528 U.S. at 141, 143-44 (2000), *available at* http://laws.findlaw.com/us/000/98-1464.html (noting Congress' finding that many states have historically sold information from their drivers' license records to businesses and individuals) (citing 139 Cong. Rec. 29466, 29468, 29469 (1993); 140 Cong. Rec. 7929 (1994) (remarks of Rep. Goss)).

As discussed above, the digitization of state records has vastly improved the usability of the information while dramatically decreasing the cost of obtaining it. While this new potential has drawbacks, commentators have noted that eliminating practical obscurity can be of enormous benefit to consumers.[93] Cheaper, more accurate information about potential customers can reduce the cost of doing business and allow consumers to receive solicitations that are better targeted to their interests and income, rather than randomly-generated mailings.[94] Thus, the Direct Marketing Association asserts that more accurate consumer information actually decreases the amount of unwanted telephone and mail solicitations while giving consumers more information and access to a greater variety of products and services at a reduced cost.[95] Put simply, consumers benefit when the businesses they use spend less to make better decisions.[96]

5. Tax-Reducing Opportunities

Public records have value to various businesses and individuals and many states charge a fee for access to their records. The revenue collected from this sale of public information can be significant. For example, prior to the passage of the federal Drivers Privacy Protection Act, the Wisconsin Department of Transportation received approximately $8 million per year from the sale of drivers license data.[97] This supplemental income can allow states either to reduce taxes or increase the services they provide to their citizens.

6. Public Safety

Law enforcement relies on public records to fight crime. According to FBI Director Louis Freeh, information from public record sources "assisted

[93] *See, e.g.*, Singleton, *supra* note 21 (noting the economic benefits of the free flow of personally-identifying data but arguing that such data is less problematic when gathered and maintained in private, rather than state, databases).

[94] *See* Michael A. Turner, A Call to DMA Members ... Address Your State Lawmakers (Mar. 13, 2000), *at* http://www.the-dma.org/cgi/dispnewsstand?article=82+++++++.

[95] *See id.*

[96] *See* Cate, *supra* note 90, at 28-29. Paul H. Rubin & Thomas M. Lenard, *Privacy and the Commercial Use of Information* (2001).

[97] *See Condon*, 528 U.S. at 143-44, *available at* http://laws.findlaw.com/us/000/98-1464.html (citing *Travis v. Reno*, 163 F.3d 1000, 1002 (7th Cir. 1998)).

in the arrests of 393 fugitives wanted by the FBI, the identification of more than $37 million in seizable assets, the locating of 1,966 individuals wanted by law enforcement, and the locating of 3,209 witnesses wanted for questioning."[98]

Federal, state, and local governments have long published selected personally-identifying information about their citizens in an attempt to promote law enforcement and enhance public safety.[99] A prominent example is the FBI's use of suspects' names, photos, fingerprints, and other descriptive information on its "10 Most Wanted" posters. The FBI now posts its "Most Wanted" information on the Internet, as well as in the customary locations such as post offices and police stations.[100]

As part of their digitization efforts, states and other governments are now making this personally-identifying information available in electronic form. The federal government and a number of states have also adopted versions of "Megan's law," making the states' records about the identity and residence of certain types of criminal offenders available to the public.[101] While some states restrict this information (which includes the names and current addresses of sexual offenders) to certain groups of citizens such as an offender's neighbors, many states have concluded that broad access promotes public safety. Therefore, they provide unrestricted access to searchable databases of this information via the Internet.[102]

7. Identity Verification

Public records can be used to verify identity, thereby helping prevent identity fraud and other crimes, while improving the accuracy of information used by legitimate businesses to make credit and other decisions. Indeed, reliable identity verification is a key part of allowing individuals access to records about themselves maintained by public and private information collectors. Such "access" is one of the core fair information principles articulated by the Federal Trade Commission.

[98] Cate & Varn, *supra* note 79 (quoting FBI Director Louis Freeh).
[99] *See* Cate, *supra* note 90, at 29 (noting that privacy may threaten safety because it impedes the public's ability to gather information about potential threats).
[100] *See* FBI, Most Wanted Web Site, *at* http://www.fbi.gov/mostwanted.htm.
[101] *See* Klaas Kids Found., Megan's Law in All 50 States, *at* http://www.klaaskids.org/pg-legmeg.htm (last modified Oct. 1999) (identifying the status of Megan's law legislation in the fifty states and providing links to state-operated databases of registered sex offenders).
[102] *See id.*

B. PUBLIC CONCERNS ABOUT ACCESS TO PUBLIC RECORDS

Despite the well-established benefits flowing from access to public records, there has been a wave of privacy-related anxiety, especially about access to electronic data.[103] In numerous books, articles and broadcasts, commentators and the media have expressed concern that the elimination of practical obscurity is having undesirable consequences. Reports have it that the public shares this worry.[104]

1. Crime

Perhaps the most motivating concern is the fear that ready access to citizens' personally identifiable information will put them at risk of crime. In addition to identity fraud, there have been several well-publicized incidents where individuals have been hurt by someone who obtained information about them from public or private databases. For example, the DPPA was passed after the 1989 murder of actress Rebecca Schaeffer, whose assailant was able to obtain her otherwise-unlisted address from her California driver's license records.[105] (It should be noted, however, that since the murderer hired a private investigator to obtain the information, the information would

[103] At least one commentator has noted that many worry who are worried about the impact of e-records do not differentiate between privacy in commercial and governmental records. *See* Singleton, *supra* note 21. At least some of this failure to discriminate among databases is justified because private and state databases can present similar threats. However, to the extent that state e-records are different from their private counterparts, we will focus on the public's concerns as they relate to the government's data.

[104] *See, e.g.*, Health Privacy Project, Study Shows Majority of Internet Users Concerned About Online Privacy (Nov. 29, 2000), *at* http://www.healthprivacy.org/info-url_nocat2303/info-url_nocat_show.htm?doc_id=41778); Bob Sullivan, *Hospital Confirms Hack Incident*, MSNBC, Dec. 7, 2000, *at* http://www.msnbc.com/news/499856.asp?0cm=c30 (reporting that a computer hacker broke into the University of Washington's computer systems and stole thousands of private medical records); Bob Sullivan, *Online Privacy Fears Are Real*, MSNBC, Dec. 6, 2000, *at* http://www.msnbc.com/news/491587.asp (discussing a number of incidents that have fueled public concerns about e-privacy); Rothfeder, Jeffrey, *Privacy For Sale: How Computerization Has Made Everyone's Private Life An Open Secret* (1992).

[105] *See* Brief Amici Curiae of the Feminist Majority Foundation, *Reno v. Condon*, 528 U.S. 141, No. 98-1464, 1999 WL 503879, at *17 (U.S. 2000) (discussing the facts of the Schaeffer murder and its impact on the passage of the DPPA).

have been available even after passage of the DPPA since the law allows private investigators continued access to DMV records.) In 1999, an assailant murdered New Hampshire resident Amy Boyer after obtaining her work address and Social Security number from an Internet search service.[106] (Though the Internet and information services are widely believed to have a proximate link to the crime, the murderer had gone to school with her, he already knew her home address, and he had stalked her for years.) In 1996, a reporter seeking to test criminals' access to personally identifiable information used the name of a convicted child murderer to obtain the names and addresses of 5,000 school children from a commercial list seller.[107] And in early 1994, a woman named Beverly Davis was harassed by a convicted rapist who had been employed to enter personal data in a private database while he was in prison.[108] Additionally, a number of government agencies have faced allegations that employees who have access to the agency's databases for legitimate purposes improperly use that access to view personal information about other employees or acquaintances.[109]

2. Annoyance

Even where crime is not an issue, many citizens want to restrict access to their names, addresses, and phone numbers for the purpose of avoiding the calls and correspondence of direct marketers. This is, in a way, the flip side of one benefit of access to state records. While more and better information allows marketers to more accurately determine who would be interested in hearing about their products and services, many consumers claim not to want to hear about *any* products or services at their home. This feeling is so strongly held by some that a number of laws have been enacted and several services have arisen to assist consumers in blocking contact from direct marketers.[110]

[106] *See* Sullivan, *Online Privacy Fears Are Real*, *supra* note 104.

[107] *See* Singleton, *supra* note 21 (citing *Privacy in Cyberspace*, WASH. POST, Sep. 2, 1996, at A22, and *Metromail Stung Again*, PRIVACY TIMES, May 17, 1996, at 4).

[108] *See id.* (citing *Class-Action Suit Targets Companies' Use of Prisoners*, PRIVACY TIMES, May 17, 1996 at 5-6, and Nina Bernstein, *Personal Files via Computer Offer Money and Pose Threat*, N.Y. TIMES, June 12, 1997, at A1.).

[109] *See, e.g.*, *Workers say VA violated privacy*, DALLAS MORNING NEWS, Nov. 3, 2000, at 6A (reporting that Department of Veterans Affairs employees filed suit under the federal Privacy Act alleging that the VA allows employees and some patients to access VA employees' Social Security numbers and dates of birth).

[110] *See, e.g.*, *Rowan v. United States Post Office Dep't*, 397 U.S. 728 (1970) (upholding the constitutionality of a law granting persons a right to have the Postmaster block delivery of

3. Privacy for Privacy's Sake

Privacy is also invoked as its own virtue: privacy for privacy's sake. Some simply do not want the state to reveal personal data to others regardless of whether the resulting use of that information will be beneficial or injurious.

A recent suit provides an example of how privacy can be valued as its own virtue and demonstrates how this concept of privacy can conflict with the purposes of state open access laws. In Exeter, New Hampshire, public school officials decided against using Internet filtering or blocking software on school computers, preferring to monitor students' Internet access through general supervision and spot-checks. Fearing that this approach might be ineffective in preventing his children and their peers from viewing obscene materials, James M. Knight requested that the school district allow him to view the school's Internet history files, which register the sites a particular Internet browser has visited. Mr. Knight intended to use these files to check the effectiveness of the school's Internet-supervision program (thus invoking one of the hallmark justifications for open access—monitoring the effectiveness of government policies).[111] The school district denied his request on the ground that allowing him to view the Internet history files would violate the students' privacy. Mr. Knight then filed suit, asserting that the school's tracking files are public documents and thus are open to public inspection under New Hampshire's broad Right-to-Know law.[112] A Superior Court judge ordered the school to turn over the Web logs.

---

mail from particular senders), *available at* http://caselaw.lp.findlaw.com/scripts/getcase.pl?navby=case&court=us&vol=397&page=728); http://www.junkbusters.com (providing advice and services for blocking the receipt of mass mailings and telemarketing calls). The Direct Marketing Association runs two services, the Mail Preference Service and the Telephone Preference Service, which allow consumers to remove their names from direct marketing lists. *See* http://www.the-dma.org/consumers/consumerassistance.html.

[111] *See, e.g.*, Philip T. McLaughlin, Attorney Gen., Memorandum on New Hampshire's Right-to-Know Law, RSA Chapter 91-A (May 10, 1999), *at* http://www.state.nh.us/nhdoj/Right%20to%20Know.HTM (stating that the principles underlying New Hampshire's Right-to-Know law are "openness and access to state and local government").

[112] *See* Carl S. Kaplan, *Suit Considers Computer Files*, CYBER L.J., (N.Y. Times Sept. 28, 2000), *at* http://www.nytimes.com/2000/09/28/technology/29CYBERLAW.html (reprinting an article from the *Cyber Law Journal*).

4. Property Right in Personal Information

States, businesses, and others who maintain information databases believe that those databases belong to them.[113] This is the rationale behind the long-established market for mailing lists and consumer data, and it provides an incentive for businesses to develop and maintain databases. However, a relatively novel justification for limiting access to public records is that a person has a continuing property interest in information about themselves. Thus, when a person discovers that a database proprietor has sold his or her name and phone number, information about buying habits, or any other tidbit, they might ask how that proprietor could be allowed to sell "my" personal information.[114] Or, as Solveig Singleton has put it, "[o]pponents of private databases and direct marketing assert that those who collect consumer information *steal* the information from its rightful owners. . . . Others make a similar argument, couched in softer terms, that customers should have a 'right to choose' whether their information is collected. Under that view, privacy should be an 'assignable right.'"[115]

Under this theory, information about each individual belongs to that individual even when another holds it. Accordingly, information should not be transferred without the subject's consent — even if the purpose of the transfer is beneficial to the parties or the public.

5. Embarrassment

As the volume and type of information gathered by the states grows, so does the potential that the states' records will contain embarrassing information. From health care records to crime files to traffic reports, the states' archives may contain many details about an individual's activities that

[113] *See, e.g.*, *United States v. Miller*, 425 U.S. 435, 441-43 (1976) (concluding that a bank's records of a customer's transactions belong to the bank, not the customer).

[114] *See. e.g.*, David G. Post, Privacy, Property, Cyberspace (Nov. 1997), *at* http://www.temple.edu/lawschool/dpost/privacy.html (arguing that "the law should recognize and give individuals a *property* right in personal information about themselves"); Lawrence Lessig, *Code and Other Laws of Cyberspace* 159-63 (2000) (discussing the privacy-as-property model).

[115] Singleton, *supra* note 21 (citing Esther Dyson, *Labels and Disclosure Part II: Privacy* 4 (Release 1.0 Feb. 19, 1997), and Ram Avrahami, *My Name Is Not for Sale*, L.A. TIMES, Feb. 5, 1996, at B5).

the individual would rather not have disclosed. Thus, for many the potential of public embarrassment is a drawback to accessible state records.

6. Financial Burden on the State

Although digitization of state records is intended to reduce the state's costs and often has that effect, the association of states' existing open access laws with digital recordkeeping can actually place extra burdens on the state. For instance, costs and aggravation may be increased when a state's open access law provides a right for the public to view correspondence among state officials or employees. When such a request is tendered in the digital age, the state may be required to make a search of all of the e-mail on the state's computers and electronic storage devices and produce the responsive documents. In this scenario, responding to a request for access can be cost-prohibitive. Additionally, if state officers and employees are allowed to use their computers for incidental personal e-mail, a request for a search of the state's e-mail records can raise privacy issues and related litigation.[116]

7. Generalized Uncertainty

Finally, it is worth noting that some of the public's concern regarding access to public records appears to flow from a generalized uncertainty about how such records could turn out to be used to impact individuals' lives. While this feeling is less documented, there is at least anecdotal evidence that some citizens don't want others to have information about their personal lives or contact data because they don't know why the information is wanted or what might be done with it.[117]

Courts have generally taken a case-by-case approach to defining "public record" where there is doubt and the circumstances are sensitive. For example, the Ohio Supreme Court in *State ex rel. McCleary v. Roberts* concluded that a Department of Recreation database of names of children

[116] *Tiberno v. Spokane County*, No. 18830-2-III (Wash. Ct. App. Dec. 14, 2000), *available at* www.courts.wa.gov/opinions/opindisp.cfm?docid=188302MAJ.

[117] *See, e.g.*, Alan Sipress, *"Big Brother" Could Soon Ride Along in Back Seat*, WASH. POST, Oct. 8, 2000, at A1, *available at* http://www.washingtonpost.com/ac2/wp-dyn/A32083-2000Oct7?language=printer (noting the development of increasing sophisticated state and commercial data-gathering equipment and reporting citizens' concern about their lack of knowledge regarding how the information might be used).

using the city's recreation facilities did not constitute a "record" subject to public disclosure.[118] Performing *ad hoc* balancing, the court concluded that "to the extent that any item contained in a personnel file is not a 'record,' i.e., does not serve to document the organization, etc., of the public office it is not a public record and need not be disclosed." Nothing about children's names, home addresses, parents' names, or medical information serves to document any aspect of the city's official business. The court observed that while official information sheds light on a public purpose, no such purpose is furthered by disclosure of information about private citizens that is accumulated in various governmental files. The important public interest of ensuring governmental accountability was not advanced by disclosing information the government merely happened to be storing in this case.

Though case-by-case analysis is not appropriate or required in every instance, it is a natural approach for a policy question that has many considerations lined up on both sides. It is not impossible to reconcile the competing interests weighing on public records privacy policy in a categorical way, but that task is made more complex by the rapid change from largely analog government to digital government. Electronic government, by eroding "practical obscurity," causes important shifts in how the factors going into public records policy are compared and weighed.

[118] 725 N.E.2d 1144 (Ohio 2000).

Chapter 4

Public Records and Electronic Government

Electronic government is the delivery of government information and services online through the Internet or other digital means. Many public agencies at the local, state, and federal levels have embraced the digital revolution by posting voluminous materials online and making actual government services available electronically.

As Governor of Texas, President George W. Bush and the members of the Texas Electronic Government Task Force established a new gateway to government services available 24 hours a day, 7 days a week on the Internet. Then-Governor Bush said:

> The use of technology is changing the way the government does business in Texas. The secure, one-stop Web site — the first phase of Texas' e-Government initiative — provides access to Texas government services 24 hours a day, seven days a week. Visitors can renew certain licenses and certifications, apply for permits, and much more. TexasOnline will enhance Texas government by making it more accessible, efficient, and responsive to all Texans.[119]

One of the key features of the Internet is the capability it creates to tailor goods, services, and information to the specific interests of individuals on a mass scale. The December 2000 *Report of the E-Texas Commission* is a thoughtful treatment of online customization in the realm of state government.[120] Unfortunately, the report finds that "Governments have done little to meet or even acknowledge the demand for customized service. Yet as expectations continue to rise, people will want more personalized service

[119] Statement of Gov. George W. Bush, *at* http://texasonline.com (last visited Nov. 12, 2000).
[120] E-TEXAS COMM'N, *Personalized Attention: Customized Government*, *in* REPORT OF THE E-TEXAS COMMISSION (Dec. 2000), *available at* http://www.e-texas.org/report/ch03/.

from their Governments." With considerable insight, the report notes that "a fundamental assumption behind modern Government is that all persons — all 'clients' — should be treated the same. . . . Yet the personalization trend is *precisely* about being able to treat people differently, according to their own needs and preferences. Many private companies have recognized this as the most effective way to build trust and establish long-term relationships with customers and Government should take note of their successes."[121] The Texas report notes that citizens will soon no longer be willing to wade through information in which they are not that interested in order to get the information they do want.

States like North Carolina and Virginia have introduced customizable "MyGov" web pages allowing citizens to choose from a number of topics, including public meeting announcements, interactive government service, legislative sites, local government, local media, local public schools, lottery numbers, press releases, state government, and traffic information. Donald Upson, Virginia's Secretary of Technology, has said:

> "the future is the intelligent Web site . . . . It's not just about information being available online, it's about citizens being able to tailor a 'MyGov' Web page to fit their needs. They'll be notified when their driver's license is about to expire. They'll be notified when their fishing license is about to expire. And they'll be able to handle all of those things over the network and never go to a government office at all."[122]

Of course, as Web sites are customized to take account of individual preferences and interests, they will trigger new privacy implications. Information citizens provide to the government in order to personalize their Internet interactions in essence will disclose more personal information that is not strictly necessary for the government's discharge of its official duties. It will add to the wealth of personal information that governments hold, and encourage the inter-connection of the state databases now moving into digital formats. These electronic databases are creating new concerns and drawing attention afresh to public records privacy.

[121] *Id.*
[122] *Id.*

A. THE END OF PRACTICAL OBSCURITY

For the most part, our Constitution and laws have served us well as new technologies have arisen. Nonetheless, the intersection of the physical and virtual worlds has challenged our notions of privacy. In 1928, for example, the Supreme Court ruled in the *Olmstead* case that wiretapping without a search warrant was permissible because tapping a phone involves no invasion of the suspect's physical property. Justice Brandeis, however, dissented and admonished his brethren to recognize that the Constitution's protections had to be adapted to advances in technology. He warned that "[d]iscovery and invention have made it possible for the Government, by means far more effective than stretching upon the rack, to obtain disclosure in court of what is whispered in the closet."[123] It was not until 1967 that the Supreme Court decided that Justice Brandeis was correct after all.[124]

Electronic government is the trajectory of modern life. The convenience and efficiency of providing services and information electronically is irresistible not only to budget conscious legislators, but also to citizens who want what they want, when they want it, with a minimum of hassle. But while electronic efficiency seems so much a feature of the present, it is easy to forget that computers have been around for decades. While the pace of digitization is rapid, it is not a wholly new and unanticipated development. Thus, in 1977's *Whalen v. Roe*, the Supreme Court wrote:

> We are not unaware of the threat to privacy implicit in the accumulation of vast amounts of personal information in computerized data banks or other massive government files. The collection of taxes, the distribution of welfare and Social Security benefits, the supervision of public health, the direction of our Armed Forces, and the enforcement of the criminal laws all require the orderly preservation of great

[123] *Olmstead v. United States*, 277 U.S. 438, 473 (1928) (Brandeis, J., dissenting).

[124] *Katz v. United States*, 389 U.S. 347, 350-51 (1967); *Olmstead*, 277 U.S. at 473 (Brandeis, J., dissenting). *See also Kyllo v. U.S.*, 533 U.S. __ (2001)("It would be foolish to contend that the degree of privacy secured to citizens by the Fourth Amendment has been entirely unaffected by the advance of technology."), slip op. at 6. "We think that obtaining by sense-enhancing technology any information regarding the interior of the home that could not otherwise have been obtained without physical 'intrusion into a constitutionally protected area,' . . . constitutes a search – at least where (as here) the technology in question is not in general public use." *Id.* at 6-7.

> quantities of information, much of which is personal in character and potentially embarrassing or harmful if disclosed. The right to collect and use such data for public purposes is typically accompanied by a concomitant statutory or regulatory duty to avoid unwarranted disclosures.[125]

Justice Brennan stated the point succinctly in his concurring opinion. He said, "The central storage and easy accessibility of computerized data vastly increases the potential for abuse of that information." Indeed, the Privacy Act of 1974 was passed largely out of concern over the impact of computer data banks on individual privacy.

More recently, the 1989 *Reporters Committee* decision has become a legal touchstone for privacy in the computer age.[126] The Court recognized a privacy interest in public record information that is available through other means, but that is *"practically obscure."* To the extent a "divulged" fact was intended for limited or restricted use, it would not be "freely available to the public" and could still be classified as "private" for purposes of the Freedom of Information Act. "Recognition of this attribute of a privacy interest supports the distinction, in terms of personal privacy, between scattered disclosure of the bits of information contained in a [criminal] rap sheet and revelation of the rap sheet as a whole." The Court homed in on the issue of "whether the compilation of otherwise hard-to-obtain information alters the privacy interest implicated by disclosure of that information."

The Court concluded that computerization of information does in fact make a difference:

> Plainly, there is a vast difference between the public records that might be found after a diligent search of courthouse files, county archives, and local police stations throughout the country and a computerized summary located in a single clearinghouse of information.

Privacy interests may continue to exist "even where the information may have been at one time public." The fact that "an event is not wholly 'private' does not mean that an individual has no interests in limiting disclosure or dissemination of that information." The Court then turned to its "practical obscurity" guide post and said:

[125] *Whalen v. Roe*, 429 U.S. 589, 605 (1977) (footnote omitted).

[126] *Reporters Comm.*, 489 U.S. at 763-64, 766-67, 770, 780 (footnotes and citations omitted).

> The privacy interest in maintaining the practical obscurity of rap-sheet information will always be high. When the subject of such a rap sheet is a private citizen and when the information is in the Government's control as a compilation, rather than as a record of "what the government is up to," the privacy interest protected by [FOIA] is in fact at its apex while the FOIA-based public interest in disclosure is at its nadir.

Judicial sensitivity to computers, digital databases, and privacy has thus been well characterized for years. It is not a brand new concern. Nonetheless, the issue remains acute in the minds of today's public policy makers. For example, former President Clinton stated in his May 14, 1998 memorandum "Privacy and Personal Information in Federal Records":

> [i]ncreased computerization of Federal records permits this information to be used and analyzed in ways that could diminish individual privacy in the absence of additional safeguards. As development and implementation of new information technologies create new possibilities for the management of personal information, it is appropriate to reexamine the Federal Government's role in promoting the interest of a democratic society in personal privacy and the free flow of information.[127]

Similarly, the ramifications of the Internet and electronic access to personal information have stimulated much thoughtful analysis within numerous state governments.

In its excellent report, *Privacy Issues Involved in the Electronic Government*, the Texas Department of Information Resources noted that whereas documents were traditionally filed away in warehouses or buried in the file cabinets, the Internet makes access to public information extremely easy. With convenience comes problems arising from the sale or improper distribution of personal information. The report notes that what makes *data* different from physical objects is the ease with which data can be sold or distributed through the various media of the electronic society. "The

[127] Memorandum from President Clinton, to the Heads of Executive Departments and Agencies, Privacy and Personal Information in Federal Records (May 14, 1998), *available at* http://www.whitehouse.gov/omb/memoranda/m99-05—a.html.

ramifications of having widespread knowledge of data are immense. One's medical and financial records could be used in hiring decisions. Social Security numbers could be used in crimes of identity theft and financial fraud. Something as public as one's address could be used to conduct a hate crime."[128] Moreover, once information is released electronically, it becomes nearly impossible to protect it in the future. Released information can be bought, sold, and disbursed widely without knowing exactly who holds the information and how they are using it.

Washington State, home of Microsoft and numerous high technology and Internet companies, has been especially attuned to the intersection of computers and privacy. In November 2000, Governor Gary Locke stated that "the explosion of computerized databases around the world requires that we protect personal information, such as Social Security numbers, as fully as possible. At the same time, we will continue to make public information about state government and its operations available as quickly and conveniently as possible."[129]

The end of "practical obscurity" challenges public records policy, but it is important to recognize how delicately balanced it is as we examine how to modernize our approach to the tension between access and privacy.

B. MODERNIZING PUBLIC RECORDS PRIVACY POLICY

In modernizing public records privacy policy, there are a few basic principles that are appropriate to start with. First, there exists a delicate balance among our constitutional ideals of open government and personal privacy; this counsels against radical changes in information policy.

Second, it would be a mistake to adopt overly prescriptive and inflexible new restrictions on access to public records at a time when electronic government initiatives — and the power of electronic media to benefit society — are at a relatively early stage of their evolution.

Third, a great deal of very sophisticated thinking and action has already taken place to reconcile the dual social goals of disclosure and withholding of public records containing personally identifiable information. Indeed, the now well known "fair information principles" — notice, choice, access, and

[128] TEX. DEP'T OF INFO. RES., *supra* note 80, at *Introduction*.

[129] Press Release, Office of Gov. Gary Locke, 74 Agencies and institutions comply with Locke's privacy executive order (Nov. 8, 2000), *available at* http://www.governor.wa.gov/press/2000/00110802.htm

security — were first laid out over a quarter of a century ago in a 1973 report prepared for the Department of Health, Education and Welfare (now Health and Human Services). The report, *Records, Computers, and the Rights of Citizens*, was prepared by an advisory committee on automated personal data systems.[130] It significantly influenced the 1974 Federal Privacy Act.

Since then, of course, the Federal Trade Commission (FTC), and numerous other governmental and self-regulatory organizations have adopted, adapted, and elaborated upon these core fair information principles. These principles were summarized in the FTC's 1998 report, "Privacy Online: A Report to Congress."[131]

(1) **Notice** – Data collectors must disclose their information practices before collecting personal information from consumers.

(2) **Choice** – Consumers must be given options with respect to whether and how personal information collected from them may be used for purposes beyond those for which the information was provided.

(3) **Access** – Consumers should be able to view and contest the accuracy and completeness of data collected about them; and

(4) **Security** – Data collectors must take reasonable steps to assure that information collected from consumers is accurate and secure from unauthorized use.

The FTC has also identified **enforcement** — the use of a reliable mechanism to identify and impose sanctions for non-compliance with the fair information practices — as a critical ingredient in any governmental or self-regulatory program to ensure privacy online.

Many public agencies have successfully implemented these principles already in their public record practices. Many more have not. The curiously slow rate of state, county, and city adoption of Web site privacy policies is

[130] Report available at http://aspe.hhs.gov/datacncl/1973privacy/tocprefacemembers.htm.

[131] FTC, Privacy Online: A Report to Congress (June 1998), *available at* http://www.ftc.gov/reports/privacy3/index/htm.

inexcusable. Much progress is still left to be made, and the private sector's efforts have outstripped the public sector's many times over.

While respecting the delicate balance between openness and privacy, public records privacy reformers also need to be realistic. No matter how enlightened public record privacy policies may be, there is little prospect of going back to the Supreme Court's 1989 vision of "practical obscurity." This is certainly a vanishing safeguard. In almost every particular, the information revolution is auspicious for personal autonomy and private opportunity; yet, there is no denying that nearly instantaneous access to an almost limitless wealth of knowledge allows strangers to learn a great deal of once "private" information about us.

Because "practical obscurity" is fading as a viable safeguard, it would be a serious mistake to design public record privacy policy around it. Once any piece of information becomes available anywhere in the public domain, its obscurity is effectively lost forever. Public agencies should therefore not pretend that their privacy policies can guarantee or preserve a "practical obscurity."

However, the loss of obscurity does not necessarily portend the end of privacy as we know it. Nor should we develop convoluted, new privacy criteria for digital, electronic, and online media. Rather, public records policy needs to identify categories of particularly sensitive information and protect those particular categories assiduously. They must keep confidential truly sensitive information — identifying account numbers, health information, children's names, and the like. Public agencies should concern themselves with protecting types of content, rather than obsessing about the risks of digital processes or formats.

In the same vein, public records policy should avoid moving in a direction where "who asks" for the information determines whether they can get it. Some courts have, unfortunately, allowed legislatures and public agencies to discriminate among different requestors of information (commercial, media, individuals) and to condition access to public information on the basis of intended uses.[132] (Fortunately, this error is not permissible under the Federal Freedom of Information Act.)

The Supreme Court's 1999 decision in *Los Angeles Police Department v. United Reporting Publishing Co.* offers a concrete example of requestor and use discrimination. That case involved a California statute that placed two conditions on public access to government records containing the addresses of arrestees. The person requesting an address was required to declare that the request was being made for one of five specifically permitted purposes

[132] *Los Angeles Police Dep't v. United Reporting Publishing Co.*, 528 U.S. 32 (1999).

and that the address would not be used directly or indirectly to sell a product or service.

The Los Angeles Police Department maintained records relating to arrestees. The requestor, United Reporting Publishing Corporation, was a private publishing service that provides the names and addresses of recently arrested individuals to its customers, including attorneys, insurance companies, drug and alcohol counselors, and driving schools. United Reporting could not "declare[ ] under penalty of perjury" that it was requesting information for one of the prescribed purposes and that it would not use the address information to "directly or indirectly . . . sell a product or service," as the statute required.[133]

The Supreme Court upheld the California requestor and use discrimination statute on technical legal grounds. But Justice Ginsburg, in her concurring opinion, provided a substantive rationale in support of allowing California to discriminate among requestors and potential uses of information. Her pro-discrimination view was not repudiated in either the majority or dissenting opinion. She wrote:

> California could, as the Court notes, constitutionally decide not to give out arrestee address information at all. It does not appear that the selective disclosure of address information that California has chosen instead impermissibly burdens speech. To be sure, the provision of address information is a kind of subsidy to people who wish to speak to or about arrestees, and once a State decides to make such a benefit available to the public, there are no doubt limits to its freedom to decide how that benefit will be distributed. California could not, for example, release address information only to those whose political views were in line with the party in power. *Cf. Board of Comm'rs, Wabaunsee Cty.* v. *Umbehr,* 518 U. S. 688 (1996) . . . (local officials may not terminate an independent contractor for criticizing government policy). But if the award of the subsidy is not based on an illegitimate criterion such as viewpoint, California is free to support some speech without supporting other speech.[134]

[133] *Id.* at 35.
[134] *Id.* at 43 (Ginsburg, J., concurring).

Justice Ginsburg based her rationale for the discrimination on the grounds that the state was not obligated to disclose the address in the first place, so it could decide to release the information selectively as long as the requestor's political views were not the basis for the discrimination.

Though the Supreme Court upheld the disclosure discrimination in *United Reporting*, "identity of requester" distinctions cannot be realistically maintained in a world of increasing technological convergence. More and more, everyone with a computer is a publisher and anyone with a computer is a researcher.

Discriminating among requesters will also fail to achieve the ends it seeks. Disfavored collectors of information, such as commercial resellers, will undoubtedly acquire the information anyway, but at greater cost. Imposing additional expense on particular businesses to acquire the same information that is available to other parties, like journalists or advocacy groups, seems unwarranted.[135] Moreover, differential denial of access to public information may lull government agencies and citizens into believing they have solved a problem.

Under most circumstances, neither the nature of the requestor and the purpose for which the request is made, nor the form of the data — digital, electronic, online or otherwise — should dictate whether or not to release information. It is the *nature of the information* itself that should be dispositive. If it is sensitive, personally identifiable information should just not be released.

The nature of the government record or the branch of government should also not matter. The judiciary is now debating whether access to computerized court records should be governed by different principles from those applicable to other public agencies.[136] It should not be. As discussed further below, where court records contain sensitive, personal identifying information whose disclosure would constitute a clearly unwarranted invasion of privacy, the party filing the papers should be able to flag it and petition the court to order appropriate, but narrowly tailored, withholding from general public release. No special restrictions should apply to deny public access to court files. To do otherwise would surely promote "secret" legal proceedings, flying in the face of fundamental democratic ideals.

Individuals must also take greater *personal responsibility for* information about themselves, and governments must empower them with greater

[135] *See* Eugene Volokh, *Freedom Of Speech and Information Privacy: The Troubling Implications Of A Right To Stop People From Speaking About You*, 52 STAN. L. REV. 1049 (2000).

[136] Admin. Office of the U.S. Courts, Privacy and Access to Electronic Case Files in the Federal Courts (Dec. 15, 1999), *available at* www.vscourts.gov/privacyn.htm.

knowledge about personal information gleaned from public records is used. Individuals must be provided greater information on how to expunge, correct, or narrow the flow of that personal information. Public agencies should facilitate, encourage, and cooperate in revealing and responding to individuals' inquiries regarding information about themselves in the government's hands. Agencies should establish "public records privacy" educational Web sites and consolidate and highlight access to their online privacy resources. State agency privacy contacts should be available to answer citizen inquiries and respond to complaints or requests to access or correct personal information. Simply stated, governments must help educate citizens to exercise their individual power — and responsibility — to protect themselves.

The first line of defense against unwarranted invasions of personal privacy is personal discretion. Individuals must safeguard their sensitive data themselves. Where governments compel citizens to turn over sensitive personal information, the public agency should flag the sensitive nature of the requested information and indicate how the data will be used, to whom it will be disclosed, and what the individual can do to revise, restrict, or remove the information. People must behave — and be empowered to behave — as if their privacy is important to them if they wish to preserve it.

Two areas where these issues come into especially clear focus are governments' use of social security numbers, and the posting of collect records in electronic form. In the next two sections, we examine how states, and the courts, are addressing these areas.

C. SOCIAL SECURITY NUMBERS

The question of access to public records containing Social Security numbers (SSNs) is particularly controversial and difficult. SSN misuse is a primary factor involved in identity fraud, which is considered the fastest growing financial crime in the country. According to a congressional report, it effects approximately 500,000 to 700,000 people annually.[137] The report states that in 1999 the Social Security Administration received 62,000 allegations of Social Security number misuse, and the average number of monthly allegations has been increasing. This misuse imposes significant costs on the government, the private sector, and individuals who are victims of identity fraud. The congressional report indicates that monetary losses

[137] House Subcomm. on Soc. Sec., House Comm. on Ways and Means, Subcommittee Report on HR4857, *available at* http://house.gov/socsec/106cong/hr4857/reptlang.htm.

associated with identity fraud rose from $442 million in 1995 to $745 million in 1997, a 69% increase in two years. This is a significant, modern crime and privacy problem, by any measure.

Because the SSN is such a universally used link for personal records maintained by banks, credit card companies, telephone companies and other utilities, criminals can use SSNs to impersonate others and commit fraud. The Inspector General of the Social Security Administration, James G. Huse, Jr., told the Senate Subcommittee on Technology, Terrorism, and Government Information that in Fiscal Year 1999 his agency received over 75,000 allegations of fraud, with about 62,000 of those involving SSN misuse.[138] Inspector General Huse said "the SSN is instrumental in perpetrating identity theft crimes."[139]

As discussed before, however, tougher enforcement of existing policies, rather than the adoption of new ones, may be society's best weapon to fight the problem. Under Section 408(a)(7) of Title 42 of the U.S. Code, falsely using a Social Security number with the intent to deceive is already a felony.

Social Security numbers were created in 1936 to track worker earnings and eligibility for Social Security benefits.[140] SSNs are now used extensively by private business as well as government agencies as a unique identifier for customers and citizens. Federal law does not generally restrict or regulate the use of Social Security numbers by businesses or state governments. The GAO recently issued the following information in a letter to the House Subcommittee on Social Security:

> No federal law imposes broad restrictions on businesses' use of SSNs; consequently, businesses that request SSNs as a condition for receiving services may deny such services to individuals who refuse. However, practices vary by industry. Health care providers generally request patients' SSNs, but we were told that they do not require them as a condition for treatment. In contrast, most credit card companies request clients' SSNs as a condition for extending credit and may refuse service to those who do not comply.

[138] *Hearing Before the Subcomm. on Tech., Terrorism, and Gov't Info. of the Comm. of the Judiciary, US Senate*, 106th Cong. 15 (2000).
[139] *Id.* at 17.
[140] General Accounting Office, GAO/HEHS-99-28, *Social Security: Government and Commercial Use of the Social Security Number Is Widespread* (Feb. 1999).

> States vary in whether they require an SSN as part of the application for non-commercial driver licenses.[141]

The GAO also noted that numerous states have taken steps to protect citizens' by changing whether they display SSNs on driver's licenses. GAO noted that only Hawaii still requires SSNs to be used as a driver's license number, and that state plans to discontinue the requirement next year.[142]

In the state of Washington, Governor Locke's Executive Order 00-03 (discussed in the Washington state chapter below) specifically addresses "social security numbers and other sensitive personal identifiers." Governor Locke's Executive Order directs state agencies to eliminate "to the extent practicable" the use of SSNs and other sensitive personal and financial identifying numbers from documents that may be subject public scrutiny. The Order also states that state agencies "must exercise particular care in protecting records containing sensitive and private health, financial, and other personal identifiable information about individuals, such as social security numbers." These principles seem fundamentally sound and sensitive to privacy and crime-control concerns. There is another side of the SSN equation, however, that must be considered.

The GAO expressly recognized the need to avoid undue restriction on use of SSNs. It stated that:

> While privacy concerns should not be discounted, it is important to note that the use of SSNs to link individuals to information about them enhances the administration of federal and state programs, makes credit more accessible to consumers, and allows medical care to be integrated across providers and insurers.[143]

The GAO cautioned against adopting an unduly restrictive new law regulating the use of social security number because the additional restrictions "might hamper government and businesses' ability to conduct routine business."

[141] Letter from Barbara Bovberg, Associate Director, Education, Workforce, and Income Security Issues, GAO, to E. Clay Shaw, Jr., Chairman, Subcommittee on Social Security, Committee on Ways and Means, US House of Representatives 3 (July 7, 2000) (Social Security Numbers: Subcommittee questions concerning the use of the number for purposes not related to social security (GAO/HEHS/AIMD-00-253R SSN Use Questions)).

[142] *Id.* at 4.

[143] *Id.* at 1.

Congress asked the GAO to address possible effects on businesses of restricting their use of SSNs. The agency answered with the following key observation:

> Correctly matching a specific individual to a corresponding record of information is an important concern for healthcare providers, information brokers, and credit agencies. Limits on the use of SSNs could make it harder for health care service providers to track patients' medical histories, make it less easy for employers to do background checks, and lessen the certainty with which credit information could be match to specific individuals."[144]

Stuart K. Pratt of the Associated Credit Bureaus trade association has described the social benefits of relatively unfettered access to SSNs and similar identifying information. He told the Senate Subcommittee on Technology, Terrorism and Government Information that the existing "information infrastructure" allows efficiencies in the secondary mortgage securities marketplace that save consumers an average of two percentage points on the cost of a mortgage.[145] Mr. Pratt explained that consumer credit histories are derived from information about consumer payments furnished by credit grantors and public record items such as bankruptcy filings, judgments, or liens. He noted that these types of data sources often contain SSNs. In order to maintain the accuracy and proper identification of these files, credit bureaus use SSNs, among other identifiers. To the extent that credit reports and consumer files are inaccurate or ambiguous due to faulty or impartial identification, credit approvals and other transactions are impeded or slowed. In other words, credit bureaus depend on accurately identifying individuals in order to provide fraud prevention and risk management products, credit and mortgage reports, tenant and employment screening services, check fraud and verification services, and collection services to hundreds of thousands of customers in the United States and internationally. State governments also rely on this type of information to reduce many forms of fraud in government benefit or entitlement programs.

According to the General Accounting Office's 1999 report, *Social Security: Government and Commercial Use of the Social Security Number Is Widespread*, credit bureaus and state income tax offices use SSNs as a

[144] *Id.* at 3.
[145] *Hearing Before the Subcomm. on Tech., Terrorism, and Gov't Info.*, *supra* note 138, at 72.

primary record identifier, for maintaining individual consumer credit histories, for example.

> Officials of all the organizations we contacted said they use SSNs to match records with those of other organizations to carry out the data exchanges necessary to conduct their businesses. Data exchanges are conducted for such purposes as obtaining information to asses credit risk, locate assets, and ensure compliance with program rules and regulations.[146]

Credit bureaus have said that if credit reports could not be requested using SSNs, organizations would have less assurance of receiving full and accurate information.[147]

According to GAO, businesses and government agencies ask for SSNs when individuals apply for benefits or services, including driver's licenses, credit, checking accounts and insurance, apartment rentals and public utilities.[148] State agencies use SSNs to support state government operations and offer services to residents. The Social Security Act authorizes states to use SSNs to administer any tax, general public assistance, driver's license, or motor vehicle registration law.[149] According to GAO, business and state officials told them that any federal law restricting the use of SSNs would have a negative impact on them.[150]

> [R]epresentatives of these organizations said that such restrictions could impede credit bureaus' ability to accurately post consumer payment and credit transactions and state tax agencies' ability to identify tax filers. Moreover, many of the officials . . . believed that federal restriction of their use of SSNs would hamper their ability to conduct data exchanges with other organizations.[151]

GAO found that because of privacy concerns raised by disclosure of personal information, businesses and states have already begun voluntarily restricting

[146] General Accounting Office, *supra* note 140, at 2.
[147] *Id.* at 3.
[148] *Id.* at 7.
[149] *Id.* at 10.
[150] *Id.* at 12.
[151] *Id.*

their disclosure of personal information such as SSNs.[152] As mentioned above, nearly all states have discontinued the use of SSNs on driver's licenses, and numerous states — such as Washington and Kentucky — have restricted their general disclosure of SSN information.

Of course, new legislation that would prohibit or curtail the use of SSNs by legitimate businesses and state agencies would go far beyond simply preventing those organizations from disclosing SSNs indiscriminately. The focus should, instead, be on reducing the disclosure of SSNs while preserving relatively unfettered use of SSNs by state and private organizations that need the numbers for lawful and beneficial identification and matching purposes.

The courts are already engaged in making precisely these sorts of distinctions. The U.S. Court of Appeals for the 4th Circuit has noted that "since the passage of the Privacy Act, an individual's concern over his SSN's confidentiality and misuse has become significantly more compelling. . . . The harm that can be inflicted from the disclosure of a SSN to an unscrupulous individual is alarming and potentially financially ruinous."[153] Based on this analysis, the Court of Appeals concluded that a Virginia state statute that required a voter to disclose his or her SSN for subsequent publication in voting rolls was "a profound invasion of privacy when exercising the fundamental right to vote. . . . [The citizen's] fundamental right to vote is substantially burdened to the extent the statutes at issue permit the public disclosure of his SSN."[154] Thus, Virginia could not condition a fundamental right — voting — on public disclosure of an SSN.

Similarly, the Ohio Supreme Court found that privacy limitations under the U.S. Constitution weigh against indiscriminate disclosure of the SSNs of city employees. Because of "the high potential for fraud and victimization caused by the unchecked release of city SSNs outweighs the minimal information about governmental processes gained through the release of the SSNs . . . . [W]e conclude that the United States Constitution forbids disclosure under the circumstances of this case. Therefore, reconciling federal constitutional law with Ohio's Public Records Act, we conclude that [the provision] does not mandate that the City of Akron disclose the SSNs of all of its employees upon demand."[155]

More recently, the U.S. Court of Appeals for the 5th Circuit upheld the U.S. Army's decision to withhold SSNs from service records released under

[152] *Id.* at 13.
[153] *Greidinger v. Davis*, 988 F.2d 1344, 1353-54 (4th Cir. 1993).
[154] *Id.* at 1354.
[155] *State ex rel. Beacon Journal Publ'g Co. v. City of Akron*, 640 N.E.2d 164, 169 (Ohio 1994).

the Freedom of Information Act. The court found that the disclosure of military personnel records reflecting awards approved for individual soldiers "would constitute a clearly unwarranted intrusion into the privacy interests of army service personnel" if SSNs were not redacted from the files before release. The court agreed with the Army's argument that "'social security numbers linked to individuals' names and other identifying information increasingly provide ready access to numerous personal details about an individual, creating a very real danger of identity theft and other significant intrusions on personal privacy.'" The court indicated that "the increasing prevalence of identity fraud, as reflected in various federal statutes, demands that federal agencies take particular care when publicly disclosing documents that contain SSNs."[156] On the other hand, there is a significant public interest in disclosure of SSNs, such as avoiding fraud by individuals who are filing for bankruptcy. In these cases, "the relatively low risk of identity theft may sufficiently diminish the privacy interest in SSNs to warrant their disclosure [because] a strong public interest in disclosure exists."[157]

A recent court of appeals decision considered whether a federal statute requiring an individual who helped prepare bankruptcy petitions to include his SSN on the petition violated the individual's constitutional right to privacy.[158] What the bankruptcy preparer objected to was not the government's collection of an SSN, but, rather, the subsequent disclosure of the number to the general public. Papers filed with the bankruptcy court become part of the public record. The court agreed that the indiscriminate public disclosure of SSNs, especially when accompanied by names and addresses, could implicate a constitutional right to information privacy. However, like all courts considering the "right" or "interest" in information privacy, the court in this case wrote, "The right to informational privacy, however, 'is not absolute; rather, it is a conditional right which may be infringed upon a showing of proper governmental interest.'"[159]

To determine whether the right can be infringed, courts engage in the delicate task of weighing competing interests to determine whether the government can properly compel the disclosure of private information. In most cases, the court noted, it is the overall context, rather than the particular item of information that dictates the tipping of the scales. In this case, the bankruptcy petition preparer complained that the disclosure of an SSN would

[156] *Sherman v. United States Dep't of the Army*, No. 00-20401, 2001 WL 224654, at *1, *3, *7 (5th Cir. Mar. 7, 2001).

[157] *Id.* at *6; *see also Ferm v. United States Trustee* (*In re Crawford*), 194 F. 3d 954, 959 (9th Cir. 1999).

[158] *Ferm v. United States Trustee* (*In re Crawford*), 194 F.3d 954 (9th Cir. 1999).

[159] *Id.* at 959 (quoting *Doe v. Attorney General*, 941 F.2d 780, 796 (9th Cir. 1991)).

make him vulnerable to certain crimes. "While this surely implicates Ferm's informational privacy interests, it does not appear to constitute a more serious invasion of those interests than many other requirements imposed by the government."[160] To weigh the privacy interest properly, the court felt that it was necessary to weigh the dire consequences of identity fraud against the discounted probability of its occurrence. The court allowed disclosure of the SSN in this case because "a SSN is not inherently sensitive or intimate information, and its disclosure does not lead directly to injury, embarrassment or stigma."[161] The court also concluded that the government had weighed the interest in preventing fraud through the collection of SSNs, and the disclosure of those numbers served the important purposes behind the bankruptcy code's "'public access'" provision.[162]

On May 10, 2001, the Superior Court of the State of Washington decided an important Social Security Number case involving Internet publication of personal information – including SSNs – about the City of Kirkland's law enforcement personnel. The Court allowed the continued publication of the police officers' addresses and telephone numbers, but said "Social Security Numbers are different." The Court enjoined the website operators from continuing to publish SSNs on the grounds that disclosure of this information was "highly offensive to the reasonable person" and "not of legitimate concern to the public."[163]

On balance, the very fact that state agencies and private businesses value the use of SSNs is the reason why their indiscriminate disclosure should be prevented. Legitimate organizations should be able to obtain this information from individuals and other organizations in order to match data records based on the SSN. But if identity criminals can freely harvest SSNs from public records, legitimate uses will pay the price. In the current climate of anxiety over identity fraud, the ability of organizations to continue to ask for and use SSNs should depend on whether they can assure that they will not routinely or freely disclose such information. Fortunately, even the sponsors of new legislation that would restrict public access and sale of social security numbers, like Senator Judd Gregg, recognize "that there are certain legitimate purposes for which the social security number is essential –

[160] *Id.*
[161] *Id.* at 960.
[162] *Id.*; 11 U.S.C. § 107(a).
[163] *City of Kirkland v. Sheehan*, No. 01-2-09513-7 SEA (Wash. Super. Ct. King County May 10, 2001) (politech.com) (order granting injunction), *available at* http://www.politechbot.com/docs/justicefiles.opinion.051001.htm.

and we must protect those legitimate uses."[164] Bank and financial institution use of SSNs to determine that a loan applicant is who he or she says they are – and thus prevent fraud – was specifically identified as a legitimate use by Senator Gregg.

Even though this book argues generally that requesters should not be discriminated against in obtaining information from public records, Congress' judgment that certain uses of information should be specially favored makes sense. As a general rule, the Drivers Privacy Protection Act (discussed earlier in the federal privacy chapter) prohibits state departments of motor vehicles from disclosing or making available "personal information about any individual obtained by the department in connection with a motor vehicle record."[165] However, the Act also contains 14 separate "permissible uses" that qualify the categorical prohibition on the disclosure of drivers records. One permissible use, for example, is "in the normal course of business by a legitimate business . . . to verify the accuracy of personal information submitted by [an] individual to the business." Clearly, Congress has made a judgment that legitimate businesses like insurance companies, licensed private investigative agencies, security services, and employers should have privileged access to personal information in motor vehicle records because such access is socially useful.

Certain actors in society have an interest in allowing legitimate businesses to verify the information that is submitted to them. Employers, insurers, lenders, and other such entities ought to be able to confirm the information submitted to them in order to reduce fraud and deception.

Many of these private institutions are themselves subject to significant privacy requirements. For example, the Federal Fair Credit Reporting Act, the Electronic Fund Transfer Act and the recent privacy provisions of the Gramm-Leach-Bliley Act impose certain confidentiality requirements on financial institutions and restrict the disclosure of customer information to third parties without customer consent. Because of the unique problem with identity fraud, and its close relationship to SSNs, it may be appropriate to derogate from the general rule that public records should be available to all requesters. In other words, the confidentiality statutes that already apply to certain legitimate business users can, in the words of the federal district court in Washington, D.C., "address[] [the privacy] issue and eliminate[] any possible tension between" the goal of privacy and socially useful business

[164] 147 Cong. Rec. S4596 (daily ed. May 9, 2001) (comments of Sen. Judd Gregg on S. 848, "Social Security Number Misuse Prevention Act" (Introduced by Senators Diann Feinstein and Judd Gregg)).

[165] 18 U.S.C. § 2721 (a).

access to personal information.[166] Indeed, the existence of privacy safeguards – i.e., "concomitant statutory or regulatory dut[ies] to avoid unwarranted disclosures" – was precisely the factor underlying the Supreme Court's decision to uphold New York's medical disclosure statute in *Whalen v. Roe.*[167] State courts have also recognized that "the dissemination of personal information by commercial enterprises is more limited" than dissemination by other members of the public.[168] Access to court records is a closely related and significant debate.

D. INTERNET AVAILABILITY OF COURT DOCUMENTS

The Judicial Conference of the United States, the policy-making group for federal courts, is currently examining access to court records over the Internet. This debate is also being driven heavily by concern with identity fraud. The Conference is considering amending the Federal Rules of Procedure to permit posting court documents electronically to the Internet. A public comment period on the issue ended January 26, 2001, with the Conference receiving more than 200 comments. The comments are posted to the Judicial Conference's privacy web site.[169]

In general, journalists and professional groups that use public documents favor the Internet availability of documents that would normally be available to the public at a court house. Privacy advocates, on the other hand, believe some limits are appropriate to prevent privacy violations, identity fraud, and mass marketing. The Privacy Foundation has recommended that the courts develop a technologically feasible method for automatic removal of "sensitive-but-not-confidential" information, such as Social Security Numbers and medical records.[170] The Social Security Administration is also opposed to posting federal court files to the Internet. It is particularly concerned about the medical information that is contained in disability proceedings.

[166] *See Individual Reference Servs. Group, Inc. v. FTC*, Civ. Action No: 00-2087, slip. op. at 39 (ESH) (D.D.C. April 30, 2001).

[167] 429 U.S. 589, 605 (1977)

[168] *Sheehan*, No. 01-2-09513-7 SEA (politech.com), *available at* http://www.politechbot.com/docs/justicefiles.opinion.051001.htm.

[169] Judiciary Privacy Policy Comment Page, *available at* http://www.privacy.uscourts.gov/default/htm.

[170] Privacy Foundation Comment *available at* http://www.privacyfoundation.org/release/story8court/htm#comment.

In March 2001, the Judicial Conference of the United States held a hearing to discuss the desirability of posting all court records on the Internet. Naturally enough, the representatives of the Reporters' Committee for the Freedom of the Press argued for the position that public access to court records means little if the access is not meaningful. Lucy Dalgish, Executive Director of the Reporters' Committee, stated that "we believe that privacy interests are protected as necessary with protective orders." The Newspaper Association of America adopted a similar view. The Newspaper Association's President, John Sturm, observed that "the Internet offers public scrutiny of court proceedings the likes of which the founding fathers could never have imagined, but they would have supported." On the other hand, the Electronic Privacy Information Center expressed concern about unfairly stigmatizing litigants who disclose personal information in the context of judicial proceedings. The Electronic Frontier Foundation went so far as to suggest that the definition of "public record" should be redefined in the era of electronic access.

The agreements in favor of openness, however, are overwhelming. As Rene P. Milam, General Counsel of the Newspaper Association of America, said:

> Access to court records generates valuable stories about the business before the federal courts and about the functioning of the court system and government agencies as a whole, by doing so, open court records help inform our citizenry, promote the public monitoring and the accountability of the court system and in the end strengthen our democracy and the rule of law. Electronic access to federal case files . . . will multiply these benefits by making them accessible more widely, more easily, and more costly-effectively.[171]

He also noted that limiting access to public court files would be a step backward without any compelling policy reason. This argument seems almost certainly correct. As the Supreme Court noted in *Richmond Newspapers*, it is essential to open society that the public is able to obtain full access to the contents of judicial proceedings.

It is important to note, however, that Courts and judges have long experience with sealing court documents whose disclosure is inappropriate. The end of practical obscurity in court records should make judges more aware of their obligations to seal records where appropriate, but it should *not*

[171] *Available at* http://www.naa.org/about/sturm_test_comments.html.

change the standard for denying public access to judicial proceedings. Given our nation's long history of open court proceedings, the public can hardly expect generalized privacy in court filings. Where a sensitive matter must be discussed in a filing, courts and litigants should rely on the existing procedures for sealing the records or imposing protective orders.[172] It would be a grave error to sweep public proceedings under the rug in the name of privacy.

Court records and Social Security numbers are two areas of particular concern for those studying how to modernize public records policy. They are particularly affected by the erosion of "practical obscurity" as government processes and files move to digital formats. With caution and due regard for the thinking and study that have gone before, public records policy may be adjusted to address this challenge of electronic government. The examples and recommendations in the next chapter provide guidance on how this delicate task can be achieved.

[172] For example, Federal Rule of Civil Procedure 26(c) provides for protective orders to protect private information obtained in discovery.

Chapter 5

"Best Practices," Findings and Recommendations

There has been a tremendous amount of excellent analysis and insight into the best practices that state and local governments should follow to balance the public's dual interests in privacy and open access. Fred H. Cate and Richard J. Varn produced an excellent report in 1999 for the Coalition for Sensible Public Records Access (CSPRA), *The Public Record: Information Privacy and Access*.[173] The Office of Management and Budget (OMB) in the Executive Office of the President has also produced voluminous materials prescribing privacy practices for federal agencies.[174]

The State of Washington has addressed public records privacy primarily at the executive level through a sophisticated executive order and state task force reports. The State of Texas has produced enormously useful analytic and descriptive materials regarding the privacy practices of a wide range of jurisdictions within the United States and around the world.[175] Florida Governor Jeb Bush has issued an executive order convening a task force to develop new public record privacy policies.[176] True to form, the State of California appears to be the most legislatively active in the area, having adopted the California Information Practices Act in 1977.[177] That statute requires state agencies to maintain only such personal information as is relevant and necessary to the governmental purposes for which it is collected, and it provides for disclosure of personal information under specified circumstances with an opportunity for the subject to access and amend

[173] Cate & Varn, *supra* note 79.

[174] Materials available at http://www.whitehouse.gov/omb/memoranda/m99-05-a.html

[175] TEX. DEP'T OF INFO. RES., *supra* note 80, at *Introduction*; Office of the Attorney Gen. of Tex., Information Held by Government Bodies Deemed Private or Confidential by the Texas Constitution and Statutes, *at* http://www.oag.state.tx.us/notice/privacy_statutes.htm (last modified July 21, 2000).

[176] Fla. Exec. Order No. 00-235 (July 31, 2000).

[177] CAL. CIV. CODE § 1798.

records that pertain to them. The governments of Australia and Canada have also been particularly active in the subject of governmental records privacy.

The prevailing philosophy in the United States is that the public should have access to information collected by the government. "Open government" is a prerequisite to official accountability so, as important as the public's interest in privacy is, there is risk of adopting new laws too casually. The existing constitutional balance in favor of open government could be upset by over-emphasizing society's current expressions of anxiety over information privacy. Despite the volume of commentary, there is little real evidence that the substantive privacy protections existing today are inadequate. New procedural laws, however, if narrowly tailored, just might enhance both open government and public records privacy — so long as they deal with procedure more than new substantive criteria that could upset the existing balance in unpredictable ways. It is preferable for state governors to take executive action implementing many of the best practices and policies discussed here, instead of encouraging new legislation.

Thoughtful executive orders advancing a public records privacy agenda have been issued by Governor Locke of Washington, Governor Bush of Florida, and others. Governor Locke's executive order directly recognizes that state agencies should minimize as much as possible the collection, retention and release of personal information and provide citizens with broad opportunities to know what personal information about them the state holds. Citizens should have the opportunity to review and correct that information. Governor Locke directs that, to the extent practicable, each state agency must eliminate its use of Social Security numbers and other sensitive personal and financial identifying numbers from documents that could be subject to public scrutiny. He also directs that each state agency should adopt a privacy policy for the Internet Web sites they operate. Those policies should describe the manner in which the personal information is collected, the intended use of the information, a brief description of laws relating to disclosure and confidentiality of the collected information (with a link to the State Public Records Act and other laws as appropriate), the consequences of withholding information, methods for accessing the information and notifying agencies regarding the use or misuse of the person's personal information, as well as other criteria.

Governor Locke also established a "Governor's Work Group on Commercial Access to Government Electronic Records." This group, and other task forces established in Washington State, have produced excellent surveys of public records privacy, including actual assessments of agency progress on this subject.

In Florida, Governor Jeb Bush has also established a "Task Force on Privacy and Technology" by Executive Order number 00-235. This task force is charged with providing criteria for developing new identity protection and privacy policies that are consistent with both the state and federal constitutions and laws. The legislation under which Governor Bush acted directed the State Technology office to create the task force and make policy recommendations on issues such as privacy, technology fraud, and the collection, use, and release of government collected records to private individuals and companies. By calling for an investigative and analytic task force rather than enacting new substantive standards, the Legislature adopted a productive partnership between the Legislative and Executive branches to study and work out the parameters of the privacy issue.

These examples inspire the following discussion of "best practices" for public records privacy, together with the author's findings and recommendations.

A. TAKE STOCK OF CURRENT LAW

Every state appears to be genuinely committed to open government. Because this a crucial principle of good government, states should take stock of whether their public records laws are adequate, and whether they are being effectively implemented in practice. The advent of electronic government provides both opportunities and challenges for optimizing public access to government information. To that end, many States have appointed Chief Information Officers to assist implementing these objectives.

While open government laws are pervasive throughout the states, official privacy statutes are not. The 1974 federal Privacy Act provides an excellent model for states considering legislation. In particular, individuals should have the right to obtain access to information that state governments maintain about them. Every state should assure that its laws allow, and that its institutional policies and practices encourage, citizens to find out what government records say about them. State governments must make it priority to make it easy for people to get this information.

B. CATEGORIZE PERSONAL INFORMATION

Privacy acts also reinforce the "exemptions" to disclosure contained in freedom of information or open government laws. Privacy acts help flush out what disclosures constitute clearly unwarranted invasions of personal privacy. Information should be generally available, but recognized categories of acutely personal information should be effectively protected and withheld from the public domain. Numerous state statutes already operate in this manner. Kentucky, for example, bars the disclosure of Social Security numbers and Washington prevents disclosure of personal information about public school students. While it is not possible to have comprehensive lists of all information that should properly remain private, adopting a categorical approach to the kinds of information that should not be disclosed is useful to preserve the dual interest of open government and privacy. The categories of acutely personal information should be relatively narrow and easy to articulate. The more complicated the principles for withholding information from disclosure, the more likely that too much information will be kept secret.

The Federal Treasury and Justice Departments, along with the Office of Management and Budget, released a joint study on January 19, 2001, recommending that privacy protections be increased for individuals in the bankruptcy system.[178] The report provides various models for balancing privacy and access. It notes that existing federal bankruptcy laws and judicial decisions reflect a case-by-case approach to balancing access by the general public and protection of personal financial information, "with that balance weighted heavily in favor of access for the general public and parties in interest, except as to 'scandalous or defamatory' information."[179] The report recognizes that comprehensive data provided by debtors in the bankruptcy system contain sensitive personal information, such as Social Security numbers, bank or credit card account numbers, incomes, and detailed listings of individuals' medical expenses and other regular expenses. This information, if used improperly, could be used to perpetrate identity fraud and other crimes.[180] The report concludes that:

> The general public not have access to certain highly sensitive information that poses substantial privacy risks to the debtor. This information may include, among other items: Social Security numbers, credit card numbers, loan accounts, dates of birth, and bank account numbers. Similarly, [the Treasury and Justice Departments and OMB] recommend that [bankruptcy] schedules that show detailed profiles of

[178] Study of Financial Privacy and Bankruptcy (Jan. 2001).
[179] *Id.* at 23-24.
[180] *Id.* at ii.

> personal spending habits and debtors' medical information be removed from the public record. . . . [and] recommend that special attention be given to protecting information regarding entities or individuals who are not parties to the bankruptcy proceeding. This includes detailed personal and financial information regarding non-filing spouses, relatives, or business partners.[181]

Texas has also produced a thoughtful document entitled *Improve Privacy Protection for Texas Citizens* that recommends that Texas adopt a privacy act, which it does not currently have, to "help ensure that government entities do not collect more information than they need, do not misuse the information they collect, and do not disclose personal information protected by law." [182] The report suggests that a new "Texas Privacy Act should prohibit disclosure of specified categories of personal information to the fullest extent possible. Government agencies should not release Social Security numbers, bank account and credit card numbers, passwords, or other such information except under extraordinary circumstances and for a compelling state interest."

A bill introduced in the last session of the Arizona House of Representatives, provides the following definition of "Sensitive Information":

> Information obtained in a commercial context, including account numbers, access codes or passwords, current of historical account balances, purchase amounts, information gathered for account security purposes, tax identification numbers, Social Security numbers, drivers license or permit numbers, state issued identification card numbers, credit card numbers or expiration dates or information held for the purpose of account access or transaction initiation.[183]

Despite the presumption in favor of disclosure, courts have consistently protected intimate personal information that, if disclosed, could cause the individual personal distress or embarrassment. The Justice Department notes

[181] *Id* at 37.

[182] "Improve Privacy Protection for Texas Citizens," recommendations of the Texas Comptroller (December 2000), *available at* http://www.e-texas.org/recommend/ch01/eg09.html.

[183] HB 2717, State of Arizona, House of Representatives, 44th Legislature, 2nd Regular Session, *available at* http://www.azleg.state.az.us/legtext/44leg/2r/bills/hb2717p.htm.

that courts regularly uphold the nondisclosure of sensitive personal information concerning:

- Marital status
- Legitimacy of children
- Welfare payments
- Family fights and reputation
- Medical condition
- Date of birth
- Religious affiliation
- Citizenship data
- Social Security numbers
- Criminal history records (commonly referred to as "rap sheets")
- Incarceration of U.S. citizens in foreign prisons
- Sexual inclinations or associations
- Financial status

The subject of public release of lists of names and home addresses of individuals has been the subject of extensive litigation. Before the Supreme Court's 1989 *Reporters Committee* decision, courts tended to analyze "mailing list" cases based on the *purpose* for which the lists were requested. In *Reporters Committee*, the Court refused to approve withholding of information based on the identity and purpose of the requestor.

Nonetheless, courts have come close to creating a nondisclosure category for the public release of mailing lists. For example, the D.C. Circuit has concluded that mailing lists consisting of the names and home addresses of federal annuitants were categorically withholdable under FOIA's privacy exemption.[184] The Supreme Court has also twice specifically considered the issue, and held that compilations of names and home addresses of private citizens are protected under the privacy exemption.[185]

On the other hand, numerous lower courts have found little or no privacy interest in lists of names and addresses.[186] These courts have focused on the benefits that releasing such information would have as they shed light on the agency's business practices. One court, for example, ordered disclosure of

[184] *National Ass'n of Retired Fed. Employees v. Horner*, 879 F.2d 873 (D.C. Cir. 1989).
[185] U.S. DEP'T OF JUSTICE, *Exemption 6*, at 11 & n.180, *in* Freedom of Information Act Guide (May 2000), *available at* http://www.usdoj.gov/oip/exemption6.htm#exemption; *see Bibles v. Oregon Natural Dessert Ass'n*, 519 U.S. 355 (1997); *DOD v. FLRA*, 510 U.S. 487 (1994).
[186] U.S. DEP'T OF JUSTICE, *supra* note 185, at 11 n.181 (listing cases).

the names and cities of residents of Forest Service permit holders to "aid in determining whether improper influence is used to obtain permits or whether permits are being granted to those with a past history of environmental abuses." The court affirmed the withholding of street addresses because there was "no showing that knowledge of the street addresses will provide additional insight into agency activities that would not be revealed with disclosure of names and cities of residents alone."[187]

C. ESTABLISH CRITERIA FOR BALANCING

The Department of Justice's Freedom of Information Act Guide addresses the balancing process explicitly.[188] Where there is both a privacy interest in personal information and a public interest in disclosure, the two competing interests must be weighed against each other. Does the disclosure result in greater harm to personal privacy or benefit to the public? Under the "clearly unwarranted invasion" language of FOIA's privacy exemption, the scales generally tip in favor of disclosure. However, a bona fide threat to privacy need not be obvious, but must merely outweigh the public interest.

D. GIVE NOTICE TO THE PUBLIC

Some international practices, as well as the so-called "fair information principles," call for information collectors to disclose what they intend to do with information collected and what the providers of information can do to protect themselves. In general, we have not seen well-developed practices among state governments promoting disclosure of what governments will do with the personal information they receive from individuals.

Washington State Governor Gary Locke has addressed this issue directly in his Executive Order 00-03 regarding "Public Records Privacy Protections." Governor Locke states that "Each State agency that collects personal information shall, to the extent practicable, provide notice to the public at the point of collection that the law may require disclosure of the information as a public record."

This is an excellent starting point, and can be buttressed by imposing an obligation on state agency information "collectors" to determine — at the

[187] *Id.* at 11 & n.183; *see Idaho v. United States Forest Serv.*, No. 97-0230-S, slip op. at 6 (D. Idaho Dec. 9, 1997).

[188] U.S. DEP'T OF JUSTICE, *supra* note 185, at 10-15.

time they design the information collection request— whether information submitted in response to the request will be subject to disclosure or exempt under open record and privacy laws. Citizens should be advised at the time they provide information both what will happen to that information and what they can do to correct or delete information about themselves. The Internet is tailor-made to facilitate this empowerment of individuals. Hyperlinks can provide individuals with on-the-spot access to the information and officials they need to take action to protect themselves.

The primary responsibility for protecting privacy rests with individuals themselves. Americans do not always behave as though we truly value privacy, but governments must assume that we do. To that end, every reasonable tool at government's disposal should enable citizens to take control of the information that they provide and that is maintained about them in government files.

The key to protecting personal privacy, as it is to abating nearly all risks that we face in society, is personal responsibility. The responsibility of governments, in this context, is to allow individuals to protect themselves. State agencies should collect the minimum amount of information that is necessary to discharge their public purposes, and disclose to individuals whether the information the agency is collecting will be subject to public release. If the information is subject to public release, the steps that a citizen can take to revise, correct, or delete that information should be at the citizen's fingertips. Governments should empower their citizens to use official processes effectively with as few barriers or hassles as possible.

E. ESTABLISH STATE PRIVACY OFFICES AND PUBLIC OMBUDSMEN

Privacy "hotlines," ombudsman's offices, information clearing houses, and other techniques for interacting with the public are crucial to empowering the citizen. The Government of Canada's implementation of its Privacy Act is instructive. The Act establishes a fair information code requiring the government to limit its collection of personal information; to tell citizens why information is being collected and how it will be used, to provide reasonable opportunities for individuals to get access to the information about themselves; and to ensure that information is accurate and up to date. Individuals can file complaints with the Privacy Commissioner if he or she believes his or her information is not being protected in accordance with the Act, and the Commissioner is authorized to undertake investigations.

In Australia, the Office of the Privacy Commissioner (OPC) is also empowered to audit government agencies for their compliance with Australian privacy law and guidelines. This power promotes compliance and serves as an educational tool to enhance privacy protections. Almost every governmental body at the federal level in Australia has a Privacy Contact Officer to serve as an initial point of contact for the public. The OPC then coordinates the Privacy Contact Officers and oversee privacy issues. If the OPC determines that any one agency's act or practice violates the country's privacy principles, the office can order a halt to the activity.

In Hawaii, the Office of Information Practices acts as a privacy oversight agency. California also has an Office of Privacy Protection in the Office of Consumer Affairs. The California Office of Privacy Protection also serves as a central clearing house for public inquiries and complaints. In New York, the Committee on Open Government serves as an ombudsman regarding public information issues.

It is worth noting that the U.S. Department of Justice has established an Office of Information Privacy (OIP) to manage departmental responsibilities related to the Freedom of Information Act (FOIA) and the Privacy Act. It coordinates and implements policy development and compliance government-wide on FOIA issues, and handles internal Privacy Act issues for the Department. OIP decides all appeals within the Department for access to information under both Acts. OIP also maintains a website, available at http://www.usdoj.gov/oip/oip.html, where open government and privacy materials are compiled for the convenience of the public. This type of approach and office should be considered by state agencies as well.

F. ENGAGE ALL LEVELS AND BRANCHES OF GOVERNMENT

Many state legal frameworks for public records do not fully embrace public offices below the state level or in the judicial branch. This is unfortunate and has not yet been systematically addressed within the states or by many academic commentators. The California Information Practices Act, for example, applies exclusively at the state level and does not cover cities and counties. To date there is not a wealth of current "best practices" to document a recommendation on this subject. However, there is no good philosophical reason why the same principles and practices applicable at the state level should not be carried down to local government. Public records privacy principles should apply to local government offices.

State governments have also not systematically addressed judicial records. At the federal level, this is the subject of an ongoing and intense debate. As with city and county agencies, there does not appear to be any valid reason why court records should not generally be freely available to the public. The electronic age has not reduced the public's fundamental right to know what is going on in legal proceedings adjudicated by the people's official tribunals. Under existing law and practice, judges have sufficient authority to issue protective orders sealing appropriate court filings from general public view. The burden should remain on litigants to seek appropriate judicial protections for any acutely personal information whose disclosure would occasion a clearly unwarranted invasion of privacy. Withholding court filings from electronic databases, however, would strongly disserve the public's fundamental right to know.

These models provide an *executive* formula for educating the public, empowering citizens and facilitating personal privacy protections. The model action plan and public records privacy principles that follow next as the final item in this book are derived from these collective "best practices." They are offered as concrete steps and action items for state governments to consider adopting. Privacy and the Digital State will evolve over years as technology and public expectations converge. The suggestions that follow here may be of some value to smooth the process.

Chapter 6

Conclusion: A Model Action Plan and Principles for Public Information and Privacy

In the end, there is no escaping that privacy and public information are both crucial to our constitutional democracy. But neither is absolute.

This book has argued throughout that balancing and realism are necessary to develop and implement sound public policy where government records and disclosures are concerned. Moreover, while computer databases and online access to a blizzard of information portend the end of "practical obscurity," easy access to this information is plainly beneficial to society. There is no good reason to throw out decades, or centuries, of commitment to open government and public accountability simply because of computers and the Internet. Instead, government decisionmakers ought to focus on the few, relatively narrow categories of truly sensitive, highly personal information that should be withheld from publicly accessible databases. Maintaining privacy in public records should involve surgery with a scalpel, not a blunderbuss.

Even more to the point, privacy objectives must focus on real problems, not illusory ones. Therefore, preventing access to information that could lead to "identity fraud" needs to be the first priority of all public policy makers. Legislators are beginning to realize this in Washington, and state capitals should follow suit. Nothing positive is gained by diverting attention away from serious issues with well-titled legislative *nostrums* that cure nothing, but serve only to make their proponents feel good.

But inaction on privacy is not acceptable either. Based on the "best practices" surveyed for this book, there is considerable administrative potential for enhancing and refining state public information and privacy policies. The concluding pages of this book offer some basic principles and action items for consideration by state officials and those who would hold them accountable for serving the public's dual interests: getting access to useful information and protecting sensitive information to prevent clearly unwarranted invasions of personal privacy.

Most importantly, governments must face up to their obligations to empower individuals to protect their own privacy. State information collectors need to highlight when sensitive information is being collected, disclose the public access consequences of providing that information, and facilitate the public's ability to control the dissemination of their most private data. Discretion, after all, begins at home.

Of course, the privacy arena is evolving and new approaches and sensibilities will certainly arise to influence the ultimate direction of public policy. But so long as public information and privacy initiatives proceed with a recognition of society's broad interests, as well as its narrow ones, the existing constitutional balance can easily be preserved.

Model Action Plan

1. Establish a Public Information and Privacy Task Force (Governor)

2. Designate a state Public Information and Privacy Officer (Governor)

3. Appoint Governor's personal representatives, Chief Information Officer, Public Information and Privacy Officer, State Attorney General, Secretary of State, officials responsible for e-Government initiatives, representatives of county executives and city mayors to Public Records Privacy Task Force (Governor).

4. Summarize existing freedom of information acts, open records, laws and "sunshine" statutes as they relate to the disclosure of personal information (Public Information and Privacy Task Force)

5. Summarize all existing privacy and confidentiality statutes (Public Information and Privacy Task Force)

6. Index all major information systems maintained at state, county and city levels, including a chart of categories of personal information maintained (Public Information and Privacy Task Force)

7. Develop, implement and audit appropriate technological security safeguards to ensure personal information is protected commensurate with the risk and magnitude of harm that would result from the loss of misuse, or unauthorized access to such information (Public Information and Privacy Task Force).

8. Publish all summaries and indices (Public Information and Privacy Task Force)

9. Designate Privacy Contact Officers for each state agency, county and city (chief executive officer for the respective governmental units)

10. Adopt Public Information and Privacy Principles (Governor)

11. Assess adequacy of existing statutory provisions in light of Public Information and Privacy Principles (Public Information and Privacy Task Force)

12. Evaluate whether existing state privacy statutes are consistent with the Federal Privacy Act of 1974 and with the Public Information and Privacy Principles (Public Records Privacy Task Force)

13. Report on how state agencies, counties and cities share personal data with each other (Public Information and Privacy Task Force)

14. Develop a model privacy policy for each state agency, county and city for government-maintained data, including but not limited to data collected and maintained on government websites (Public Information and Privacy Task Force)

    - Each unit's privacy policy should state what personal information is collected by the agency; what use the agency makes of it; by what statutory or administrative authority the personal information is collected; to whom that personal information can be disclosed; how an individual can obtain access to the personal information collected about that individual; how the individual can amend or delete information about himself or herself; and how the unit assures that inadvertent exposure of personal data to the public or computer hackers will be prevented.

- As in Washington, the state can provide a template privacy policy that individual entities can tailor to their unique circumstances.

15. Verify that each state agency, county and city has adopted a public record privacy policy and posted it on its website (Public Information and Privacy Task Force)

16. Memorialize the activities, findings and reports of the public records privacy task force in a report submitted to the Governor (Public Information and Privacy Task Force)

17. Evaluate all future legislative proposals for consistency with Public Information and Privacy Principles (Public Information and Privacy Officer)

18. Provide for annual updating of the Public Information and Privacy Task Force report (Public Information and Privacy Task Officer)

19. Provide for periodic audits of privacy practices by state agencies, counties and cities (Public Information and Privacy Officer)

20. Investigate complaints about state agency, county or city privacy practices (Public Information and Privacy Officer; Privacy Contact Officer)

21. Develop and operate website for Public Information and Privacy Officer providing convenient, online access to all relevant reports, policies, principles, documents and contact information (Public Information and Privacy Officer)

22. Prepare an action plan to carry out the above action items (Public Information and Privacy Officer)

23. Issue Executive Order directing that the above action items be carried out (Governor)

24. Report to appropriate committees of the state legislature (Governor; Public Information and Privacy Officer)

25. Provide sufficient appropriations to fund the above action items and on-going privacy practices (state legislature)

26. Conduct oversight hearings regarding state privacy practices (state legislature)

27. Enact, if necessary, new legislative provisions respecting the balance between the public's interest in protecting personal privacy and its interest in maintaining open records and promoting government accountability (state legislature)

28. Educate the public about state privacy practices through official press releases, op-ed pieces, press interviews, and town hall meetings (Governor; Public Information and Privacy Officer; Chief Information Officer)

29. Provide for training of government employees regarding appropriate privacy practices (Public Information and Privacy Officer; Privacy Contact Officers)

Public Information and Privacy Principles

1. Personal information that would constitute an unwarranted invasion of privacy must not be released

2. Privacy interests are limited to personally identifying information; do not restrict access to public records that do not identify individuals

3. Do not release Social Security numbers, credit card numbers, bank account numbers and other financial account numbers, as a general rule unless specifically required by law

    - Recognize that society at large may benefit from allowing legitimate businesses to obtain access to such information (e.g., to prevent credit or employment fraud) provided they are subject to appropriate privacy requirements

    - Any government request that an individual disclose his or her Social Security Number must inform the individual whether disclosure is mandatory or voluntary, by what statutory or other authority the number is solicited and what uses will be made of it [Privacy Act, section 7]

4. Promote open access to government records as much as possible without harming privacy interests

5. Limit collection of personal information to what is legally authorized and reasonably necessary for the proper performance of the relevant government function, recognizing that customization of public websites to address the individual interests of citizens can be highly beneficial.

6. Restrict disclosure of personal information for the following sensitive data categories:

   - Medical records and health information
   - Tax information
   - Arrest and disciplinary proceedings not resulting in convictions or adverse dispositions
   - Names of children and minors
   - Adoption records
   - Employment records
   - Social Security Numbers and other personally identifying numbers
   - Similar information whose disclosure would constitute a clearly unwarranted invasion of privacy and be of no legitimate public concern.

7. Do not sell personal information data for a profit, but charging user fees to cover the cost of disclosure is acceptable

8. Provide individuals with access to personal information about themselves; provide reasonable opportunities for the deletion or correction of personal information consistent with law

9. Ensure security of public records so that personal information is protected from unauthorized access, corruption and destruction

10. Make public employees aware of their obligations to maintain the confidentiality of personal information and to avoid seeking or recording more personal information than is necessary or required

11. Examine record retention policies to ensure that personal information is retained only as long as necessary to carry out the purpose for which it was collected or the minimum period required by law

12. Subject government contractors handling public records to the same privacy restrictions as the public agency for which they are working

13. Approve any sharing of computer databases containing personal information between different public agencies in advance or, on a case by case basis, by the Public Record Privacy Officer

14. Encourage sharing of computer databases of personal information where it promotes greater efficiency and convenience for citizens and the agencies involved, subject to appropriate safeguards

15. Privacy Contact Officers are the first point of contact for privacy complaints made directly to an agency

16. Maintain adequate records documenting the disclosure of personal information to the subject individuals or third parties

17. Encourage electronic innovation and avoid overly restrictive practices

18. Legislative oversight should be preferred to new statutory mandates

19. Apply all privacy principles and practices to all units of state government, including the courts, as well as to all units of city and county governments

Appendix A

Privacy Practices of Selected States

The public records privacy approaches for a number of states and international jurisdictions are discussed in the pages below. Not all of the ideas described here are necessarily desirable, but the different approaches represented are nonetheless useful in designing and evaluating privacy programs for the digital state.

Though they are not summarized here, at least seven states provide a public right of access to government records or meetings in their state constitutions. Louisiana, Montana, New Hampshire and North Dakota explicitly provide a public right of access.[189] Vermont recognizes a constitutional right of access to government meetings only.[190] Tennessee and Utah have public access statutes that derive implicitly from their respective state constitutions.[191]

CALIFORNIA

California is one of only 10 states to provide a right of privacy in its constitution, which states:

> All people are by nature free and independent and have inalienable rights. Among these are enjoying and defending life and liberty, acquiring, possessing, and protecting property, and pursuing and obtaining safety, happiness, *and privacy*.[192]

[189] *See* LA. CONST. art. XII, § 3; MONT. CONST. art. II, § 9; N.H. CONST. pt. 1, art. 8; and N.D. CONST. art. XI, § 6.
[190] VT. CONST. art. VI; *see Rowe v. Brown*, 599 A.2d 333, 336 (Vt. 1991).
[191] TENN. CONST. art. I, § 19; UTAH CODE ANN. § 63-2-102(1).
[192] CAL. CONST. art. I, § 1 (amended 1972).

This provision applies to both the private and public sectors. In 1977, the state enacted its Information Practices Act, and Governor Gray Davis recently signed new privacy legislation.

Three basic statutes shape California's privacy regime in the digital age: the Information Practices Act; the Public Records Act; and the Electronic Privacy Act.

1. The Information Practices Act of 1977

The Information Practices Act (IPA)[193] applies record-keeping requirements to state agencies. The IPA does not apply to city or county governments, which may generally make their own laws in this area. Under the IPA, personal information may be disclosed to persons about whom the information pertains; relevant state agencies for appropriate purposes; law enforcement authorities, courts, and federal entities; certain relatives; and others.[194] Individuals may use the IPA to access information about themselves held by state agencies.[195] Individuals may be denied access to their records if the information involves, among other things, litigation, criminal histories, law enforcement activities, or confidential government sources.[196] On occasion, these protections have required strengthening. In reaction to the 1989 murder of actress Rebecca Schaeffer,[197] California enacted a supplementary statute to the IPA prohibiting the Department of Motor Vehicles from selling or disclosing driver's license information.[198] More recently, the Legislature passed a law eliminating general public access to voter registration records in another effort to preserve privacy.

[193] CAL. CIV. CODE § 1798.
[194] *See id.* § 1798.24.
[195] *Id.* § 1798.32. Agencies processing requests for information must respond within 30 to 60 days. *See id.* § 1798.34. Denials may be appealed in court.
[196] *See id.* § 1798.40 (2000).
[197] Beth Johnson, *A Fan's Fatal Obsession*, ENTERTAINMENT WEEKLY, July 14, 1995. The murderer had obtained the victim's address from the Department of Motor Vehicles.
[198] *See* CAL. VEH. CODE § 12800.5(a)(1). A federal version of this state law was later passed by the U.S. Congress in the form of the Driver's Privacy Protection Act of 1994 (18 U.S.C. §§ 2721-2725). The Supreme Court upheld this statute's prohibition on selling or disclosing drivers' license information (without the consent of the driver) in *Reno v. Condon*, 528 U.S. 141 (2000).

2. The California Public Records Act

The California Public Records Act (CPRA) resembles the federal FOIA and governs most records filed with state and local agencies (including cities and counties), public commissions, special districts, school districts, and other public entities.[199] Records may not be disclosed if they pertain to personnel matters; medical information; tax information; litigation; public library usage; and law-enforcement investigations.[200] In addition, electronically collected personal information is exempt from requests made pursuant to the CPRA.

3. Electronic Privacy

As part of the "Year 2000 Problem Good Government Omnibus Act of 1999,"[201] California law mandates that, by July 1, 2001, all state Web sites (including public universities) collecting personal data post privacy notices. The statute requires the privacy policies to give users detailed notice about: (1) how personal information is gathered and maintained; (2) the type of personal information collected and purpose for use; (3) the length of time that the information-gathering device will exist in the user's hard drive, if applicable; and (4) the option to have such information "discarded without reuse or distribution" after the agency is contacted post-notice to the user.[202] The law also reiterates the state's prohibition on the sale or distribution of electronically collected personal information about users to third parties without prior user consent, except where allowed in law-enforcement

[199] *See* CAL. GOV'T CODE §§ 6250-6270. Public entities must respond to requests for information within 10 days. Denials for information, along with an explanation for denial, must be issued within the 10-day period and may be appealed in court. (*See* Privacy Rights Clearinghouse, From Cradle to Grave: Government Records and Your Privacy (revised Aug. 2000), *available at* http://www.privacyrights.org/fs/fs11-pub.htm.

[200] CAL. GOV'T CODE § 6254.

[201] *Id.* § 11015.5 (2000). In addition, *see* Cal. Sec. of State Bill Jones, California eGovernment Plan: A Statewide Technology Initiative (Dec. 1999), *available at* http://www.ss.ca.gov/executive/bj_tech_plan.htm. A reference to a similar measure, called the California Electronic Privacy Act, was included in Secretary of State Jones' framework for eGovernment.

[202] CAL. GOV'T CODE § 11015.5(a)(1)-(7).

investigations (including breaches of state agency Internet networks) and by the IPA.[203]

A cursory survey of several state agency Web sites demonstrates that they were adhering to the law's prescriptions even before the final guidelines for model policies were issued in early 2001. For example, the Department of Information Technology explains the purpose and nature of the collections of personal information on its Web site:

> The only type of information that is personal in nature collected on the DOIT's web site is the IP address of those visiting the site. . . . We do not share these addresses with anyone outside of our office. Additionally, a session ID is stored in a cookie on the visitor's PC. . . . The session ID stored in the cookie upon visiting the DOITs site is randomly generated and is not being used.[204]

Meanwhile, the DMV Web site's privacy policy runs three pages, complete with technical definitions of possible identifying information and a synopsis of both how information is used and of California privacy laws.[205] The California Department of Health Services (CDHS), as another example, also hosts a fairly detailed privacy policy on its Web site.[206] However, California officials say this policy may need to be changed to reflect new requirements in federal law regarding the handling of sensitive health information.

In the past few years, officials in California formed two committee-style organizations to provide formal guidance in digital privacy.[207] In 1998, the Joint Legislative Task Force on Personal Information and Privacy led an effort to investigate digital privacy in California's state systems and to explore methods to improve privacy. The Task Force conducted hearings but produced no report. Soon afterward, the leadership of the Legislature's two chambers appointed three Senators and three Assemblymen to a special committee to examine and propose legislative measures to strengthen privacy

[203] *Id.* § 11015.5(b).

[204] *See* Cal. Dep't of Info. Tech., Privacy Policy for DOIT Website, *at* http://www.doit.ca.gov/About/privacy.asp, (last visited Oct. 28, 2000).

[205] *See* Cal. Dep't of Motor Vehicles, Privacy and Security Information, *at* http://www.dmv.ca.gov/online/vrir/privacy.htm, (last visited Oct. 28, 2000).

[206] *See* Cal. Dep't of Health Servs., Privacy Policy, at http://www.dhs.cahwnet.gov/org/home/policy/dhs-privacy_policy.htm (last visited Oct. 28, 2000).

[207] Telephone interview with Arun Baheti, Director of eGovernment, Office of the Governor, State of California (Dec. 4, 2000). Telephone interview with Lana Vierra, Legislative Aide, California Sen. Steve Peace (Dec. 4, 2000).

rights. This body's work resulted in the authorship, introduction, and passage of S.B. 129, which created the Office of Privacy Protection in the Department of Consumer Affairs.

The Office of Privacy Protection (OPP) is within the Department of Consumer Affairs and it handles consumer privacy violations, which mainly consist of identity frauds.[208] Scheduled to open January 1, 2002, the OPP will serve as the "central clearinghouse" for consumer inquiries and complaints about alleged privacy violations.[209] Such violations could conceivably involve use of information obtained from state Web sites for prohibited commercial purposes. At the present time, the California Attorney General's Office primarily handles identity frauds involving public computer networks.

The other entity charged with handling privacy policy, among other Internet issues, is the newly created Governor's eGovernment Business Advisory Council ("the Council"). The Council serves as a standing advisory commission whose membership consists of a diverse range of business leaders experienced in e-commerce issues. The Council provides continuous advice and validation for California's eGovernment efforts. For example, Council members have shared "best practices" used for consumers in the private sector with state officials to assist in creating sound policies for managing personal information.[210]

In December 2000, following passage of S.B. 129, California's Department of General Services released statewide guidelines for privacy standards on state Web sites and for government agencies in general.[211] Because of its aggressive electronic government initiatives, the state is collecting and maintaining an ever-expanding flow of personal information in digital formats. Therefore, ensuring that data remains private and used only for appropriate purposes is a top priority.

[208] According to the OPP, identity theft in California is on the rise: "In one California county alone, identity theft cases increased from 2,250 in 1998 to 3,850 in 1999, representing an increase of more than 70 percent. (*See* Press Release, Cal. Dep't of Consumer Affairs, Office of Privacy Protection Established (Oct. 2, 2000), *available at* http://www.dca.ca.gov/press_releases/20001002.htm.)

[209] *Id.*

[210] Telephone interview with Arun Baheti, Director of eGovernment, Office of the Governor, State of California (Dec. 4, 2000).

[211] *See* http://www.osp.dgs.com.gov/publications/sam/memos/mm_14.pdf. Director Baheti noted that some websites will require more detailed privacy and operational policies than others due to relevant state and federal regulations (e.g., in the areas of health care, insurance and banking). The guidelines to be unveiled will serve, in the aggregate, as a model policy containing minimum requirements. Telephone interview with Arun Baheti, Director of eGovernment, Office of the Governor, State of California (Dec. 4, 2000).

Governor Davis emphasized this point by stating in a September 2000 Executive Order that the state' electronic technology must be "secure … [and] designed to protect privacy."[212] His most significant Executive Order affecting privacy in public records and delivery of services and information is Executive Order D-17-00, which called for the implementation of electronic government.

California's privacy experience has not been without flaw. In June 1999, Governor Davis blocked the implementation of an overlooked 1998 California law that would have allowed the state's Employment Development Department (EDD) to sell confidential private salary data to banks, mortgage brokers, car dealers, and other lenders for $15 million dollars over 10 years.[213] Some private companies, including mortgage lenders, already have access to this information in paper form. The major concern arising from this episode was the ease with which an electronic database could be searched.[214] Some observers have called for the Governor to issue clear guidelines distinguishing between private information volunteered to the government that should not be disclosed and data which should be easily accessible in public records.

Another situation that aroused concerns over privacy occurred at the Division of Workers' Compensation (DWC). The DWC collects workers' compensation data on claims, cases, and benefit payments that occur in California. As part of California's electronic government efforts, the agency planned to unveil a new computer system called the Workers' Compensation Information System (WCIS) in March 2000 that would eventually digitally record all claims and activity.[215] However, on the eve of launching the program, critics (including insurers and employers)[216] warned that the system was susceptible to serious invasions of workers' privacy. This was due to the fact that, while the WCIS' regulations generally prohibited the disclosure of individually identifiable information, the measure allowed exceptions for several categories, including "statistical research."[217] According to critics of

[212] Cal. Exec. Order No. D-17-00 (Sept. 8, 2000).

[213] *See* Edmund Sanders, *Two Legislators Seek to Outlaw Sale of Salary Data*, L.A. TIMES, June 4, 1999, at C1; and unsigned editorial, *Protecting Privacy: Sacramento Must Address Consumer Concerns*, THE SAN DIEGO UNION-TRIBUNE, June 11, 1999, at B8.

[214] *Where Do We Draw the Line on Privacy?*, THE ORANGE COUNTY REGISTER, June 14, 1999, at B6.

[215] *Computer Reporting Begins, Confidentiality Questioned*, CALIFORNIA WORKER'S COMP ADVISOR (March 15, 2000).

[216] Some have observed that employers and insurers created the privacy issue to oppose the establishment of WCIS because it would reveal the fact that benefits are not often paid to workers in a timely manner. *Id.*

[217] *See* CAL. CODE OF REGS. tit. 8, § 9703(d) (2000).

WCIS, the term "researchers" could be interpreted broadly to encompass personal injury lawyers or journalists. Such a loophole could lead to serious violations of privacy, including the public exposure of an injured worker's personal health information.

FLORIDA

Florida's constitution[218] establishes a right of access to any public record made or received in connection with the official business of any public body, officer, or employee of the state, or persons acting on their behalf, except those records exempted by law or specifically made confidential by the Constitution. The right of access to public records applies to the legislative, executive, and judicial branches of government, as well as to counties, municipalities, and districts.

Florida began its tradition of openness back in 1909 with the passage of what has come to be known as the "Public Records Law"[219] and Public Records Act (PRA)[220] These laws provide that any records made or received by any public agency in the course of its official business are available for inspection, unless specifically exempted by the Legislature.

By Executive Order Number 00-235, Governor Jeb Bush established a Task Force on Privacy and Technology. The task force has studied the issues and was to make written policy recommendations in 2001. The task force is responsible for defining legal parameters for new identity-information protection and privacy policies that are consistent with the state and federal constitutions, federal law, and Florida's traditional openness under the state's laws. The task force will examine strengthening identity protection policies to address threats arising from technology and the increasing ease with which access may be gained to sensitive identity markers (e.g., medical records, credit, Social Security numbers, and personal behavioral profiles). It will also look at strengthening and or revising privacy policies relating to the collection, sharing, sale and/or release of sensitive personal and private information collected by governmental entities.

[218] FLA. CONST. art. I, § 24

[219] Chapter 119 of the Florida Statutes.

[220] Public Records Act, FLA. STAT. ch. 119.01, *available at* http://legal1.firn.edu/sun.nsf/1a9972cc30ebe40d852563cb004e9d73/d85cde087c3a681885256 6f3007272ea?.

HAWAII

Hawaii is one of the minority of states that makes personal privacy an enunciated, fundamental right in its state Constitution. The Hawaii Constitution provides:

> The right of the people to *privacy* is recognized and shall not be infringed without the showing of a compelling state interest. The legislature shall take affirmative steps to implement this right.
>
> The right of the people to be secure in their persons, houses, papers and effects against unreasonable searches, seizures and invasions of *privacy* shall not be violated . . . .[221]

Hawaii's open records law is called the Uniform Information Practices Act (UIPA).[222]

Enacted into law in 1988, the UIPA is fairly broad in scope. The UIPA outlines the statutory schemes for freedom of information, the disclosure of personal records, fair information practices, and the establishment and duties of the OIP. The freedom of information part of the UIPA operates much like the federal FOIA guaranteeing broad public access to government records except where restricted by law.[223] In general, government records that implicate a significant privacy interest may be withheld from disclosure where disclosure "would constitute a clearly unwarranted invasion of personal privacy."[224] The statute requires this balancing test for disclosure of private information held in government records: "the public interest in disclosure" must outweigh "the privacy interests of the individual."[225]

The Office of Information Practices (OIP)[226] is a state agency that acts as the watchdog of public records in Hawaii. The Governor of Hawaii appoints the Director of the OIP, which is attached to the Office of the Lieutenant Governor. The OIP implements and administers UIPA. Overall, the OIP's statutory mission is to balance the protection of personal privacy in government records with the need to ensure that the government's records and activities are open to the public. The agency holds no public records

[221] HAW. CONST. art. I, §§ 6 & 7 (emphasis added).
[222] HAW. REV. STAT. § 92F.
[223] *See* HAW. REV. STAT. § 92F-11.
[224] *Id.* § 92F-13(1).
[225] *Id.* § 92F-14(a).
[226] See http://www.state.hi.us/oip (last modified Jan. 16, 2001).

itself but instead provides assistance in gaining access to information held by the state, counties, legislative bodies, and judicial entities.[227]

OIP Director Moya Gray says the statute presumes that the public has a strong interest in making government accountable to the public. It also has a list of examples of information in which an individual has a significant privacy interest, including medical records; non-governmental employment history; information related to an individual's finances, assets, or creditworthiness; personal recommendations or evaluations; and data about an individual's eligibility for welfare benefits or social services.[228] A balancing test applies to whether private information or a document should be disclosed. A privacy interest is overridden only if the public interest in this information addresses how government operates. If the information does not address this public interest, then disclosure would be a clearly unwarranted invasion of privacy.[229]

As currently configured, the OIP has the following specific functions: (1) "fast-track" assistance; (2) legal advice, guidance and legislative review; (3) opinions; (4) education of the public; and (5) investigatory powers.[230] First, the OIP's "fast-track" assistance program offers an "Attorney of the Day" to handle requests for assistance in obtaining government or personal records as well as grievances about invasions of privacy by commercial or public parties.[231] In 2000, the OIP reported that the agency received 874 calls for assistance from individuals and other entities.[232] Second, the OIP delivers more detailed assistance through official guidance and advice in the form of opinion letters.[233] The OIP also monitors state legislation and gives annual guidance to the Hawaii Legislature and Governor for pending bills and legislative changes affecting governmental information practices.[234] Third, the OIP has issued more than 200 formal opinions and hundreds of informal opinions that comment and interpret laws on public records and privacy.

[227] Haw. Office of Info. Practices, Introduction to OIP Opinion Letters, *at* http://www.hsba.org/Hawaii/Admin/Info/info.htm (last visited Nov. 8, 2000).

[228] HAW. REV. STAT. § 92F-14(b)(1)-(8).

[229] Telephone interview with Moya Gray, Director of the Office of Information Practices for the State of Hawaii (Nov. 29, 2000).

[230] *See* HAW. REV. STAT. § 92F-41, -42.

[231] Haw. Office of Info. Practices, A Message from the Director, *at* http://www.state.hi.us/oip/dir_message.htm (last modified Aug. 4, 2000).

[232] *See* HAW. OFFICE OF INFO. PRACTICES, ANNUAL REPORT 2000, at 12 (2001). In 1999, the OIP reported 733 calls for assistance. HAW. OFFICE OF INFO. PRACTICES, ANNUAL REPORT 1999, at 4 (2000).

[233] *Id.*; *See* HAW. REV. STAT. § 92F-42(3).

[234] *See id.* § 92F-42(7).

Hawaii state courts give weight to these opinions,[235] and the Supreme Court of Hawaii has upheld the constitutionality of this process.[236] Fourth, the OIP seeks to educate the public about its rights of access and privacy related to government-retained information through public relations efforts, seminars, speakers, and training sessions.[237] Finally, the OIP may conduct investigations into agency compliance with open records laws, examine any agency's records in pursuing these inquiries, and recommend disciplinary action for agency officers.[238]

In addition, at the request of the Legislature, the OIP authored a study on the commercial use of personal information and proposed standards for governing this information in 1999.[239] Drawing from the conclusions of this study, the OIP drafted legislation that would have introduced standards to be used in the flow of certain kinds of personal information that are collected and distributed in the commercial sphere. The OIP also assisted with the coordination and drafting of Hawaii's medical privacy law, which has been enacted and will become effective July 1, 2001.[240]

To assist citizens in their research of government documents, Hawaii established the Records Report System ("RRS"), pursuant to HAW. REV. STAT. § 92F-18(b). The RRS is a computerized database that the OIP describes as "similar to a library's card catalog."[241] Currently, the RRS is accessible through a terminal located at the OIP. Depending upon availability of resources, OIP may convert the RRS to Internet access. In the RRS, researchers can find the manner of a record's storage and retrieval; contact information of the officer who holds the record; the public or private nature of the record; use categories of the record; and legal authority for maintaining the record.[242]

The OIP has adopted rules regarding access to and fees to be charged for public records.[243] It is currently in the process of drafting rules for appeals

[235] *See id.* § 92F-15(b).
[236] *See State of Haw. Org. of Police Officers v. Society of Prof'l Journalists*, 927 P.2d 386 (Haw. 1996).
[237] Haw. Office of Info. Practices, *supra* note 231.
[238] *See* HAW. REV. STAT. § 92F-42(4)-(6).
[239] *See* MOYA T. DAVENPORT GRAY ET AL., HAW. OFFICE OF INFO. PRACTICES, THE COMMERCIAL USE OF PERSONAL INFORMATION 22 (Dec. 1999), *available at* http://www.hawaii.gov/oip/privacy_report_1999.htm.
[240] *See* HAW. REV. STAT. § 323C.
[241] Haw. Office of Info. Practices, Records Report System: Identifying and Locating Public Information, *at* http://www.hawaii.gov/oip/rrs.htm (last modified May 14, 1998)..
[242] *See* HAW. REV. STAT. § 92F-18(b).
[243] *See, generally,* Haw. Admin. R. 2-71-31-33 (1999) for the newly implemented rules relating to fees. For statutory authority, *see* HAW. REV. STAT. § 92F-42(13).

from denials of requests for information; collection of personal information by government agencies; public access to research data; and safeguards for medical records.

According to the OIP, most of the components are in place for effective regulation of the collection and use of personal information: "The combination of a constitutional provision, fair information practices legislation, and an oversight agency give Hawaii the most comprehensive system of informational privacy of any state."[244] However, state legislation gives OIP more power over access issues than privacy issues. The OIP and privacy advocates in the Legislature hope to one day have in place a full-scale regime of digital privacy policy. Hawaii Governor Benjamin Cayetano, has not made any official pronouncements about privacy. However, he has created and filled a position on his staff for special adviser to the Governor on technology.

The OIP has undertaken extensive outreach efforts, aiming to educate state agencies and the people of Hawaii of the importance of protecting privacy in government records. Such education is particularly vital as information and government services move increasingly to the Internet and into the hands of business.

The OIP has adopted detailed regulations for access to public records and will adopt rules on the collection of information by government agencies. In 1999, the OIP adopted rules and response timelines for Hawaiian agencies that collect, retain and release government records, including those containing personal information. Meeting the demands of members of the public and special interest groups that inspect public documents, these new regulations introduced faster response times for certain types of documents, and articulated more clearly the procedures for handling requests for public, partially confidential and confidential records.[245] The OIP has condensed these rules into simple, comprehensive formats for visitors to the OIP website.[246] In addition, model request forms are posted on the OIP website and may be submitted via e-mail.[247] The OIP also offers guidance to the public about the operation of the UIPA on its website, including the

[244] GRAY ET AL., *supra* note 239.

[245] *See* Haw. Admin. R. 2-71-11 to -20.

[246] *See* Haw. Office of Info. Practices, A Quick Guide to the Office of Information Practices Administrative Rules, *at* http://www.state.hi.us/oip/rules_quick_guide.htm (last modified Oct. 13, 1999).

[247] *See* Haw. Office of Info. Practices, Model Forms, *at* http://www.state.hi.us/oip/rules_model_forms.htm (last modified Mar. 13, 2000).

definitions of public and restricted records, who may request records, the appeals process for denial of access, and agency responsibilities.[248]

The Hawaii State Supreme Court has before it two lawsuits that could have an impact on distribution of information via the Internet. The litigation involves Hawaii's version of Megan's Law, which is aimed at those who have committed the most serious sex offenses — violent sexual offenses and sexual offenses against minors. The law requires these sex offenders to register personally identifiable information, including name and aliases, a recent photograph, a description of the offender's vehicle, and a summary of offenses. In addition, these individuals must give notice of their whereabouts to the public by registering their addresses of residence and employment. This information is submitted to a central database maintained by the state's Criminal Justice Center. It is accessible by the public and may be accessed in electronic form through an interactive computer-based system available on the Internet.[249]

Two sex offenders sued the state over the registry, asserting violations of privacy, in addition to other challenges.[250] They argued that the mandatory registration and subsequent dissemination of personal data about all violators of certain laws undermine guaranteed privacy protections under federal and state law. A major thrust of the offenders' case is an attack on the registry's organization and accessibility. The offenders assert that the system's operation is unconstitutional because it does not discriminate in disclosing information between those offenders who present serious risks to the public and those who do not. As currently structured, the law forces an entire class of offenders — even those who do not pose the threat of committing future offenses — to forfeit their privacy even though non-threatening offenders should otherwise retain a reasonable expectation of privacy in their personal information.

Hawaii has responded to the offenders' suit by asserting that there is no reasonable expectation of privacy in the information to be disclosed under the registration statute, including publicly available information and the other items, such as fingerprints and photographs. Overall, the State has submitted

[248] Haw. Office of Info. Practices, OIP Guidance, *at* http://www.state.hi.us/oip/guidance.htm (last modified Apr. 28, 1998).

[249] HAW. REV. STAT. § 846E-3(b), (d). The database is located at http://www.ehawaiigov.org/HI_SOR/ and the front page of the Hawaii government portal website contains a link to the registry.

[250] The cases are *State v. Epps*, Crim. No. 96-1141 (Haw. filed Apr. 22, 1999) and *State v. Guidry*, Crim. No. 99-0573 (Haw. filed Aug. 5, 1999).

that the public's interest in disclosure of an offender's personal information "substantially outweigh[s] an offender's interest in privacy."[251]

Decisions on these cases are still pending in the Hawaii Supreme Court. According to some court observers, it is possible that the statute could be struck down and sent back to the Legislature for revisions along the lines of the New Jersey law.

It is too early to predict what problems Hawaii's new medical privacy law will encounter in implementation because it will not be effective until July 1, 2001. While the health care industry is rapidly preparing for the law, insurance and employer interest groups have expressed concerns and confusion about the law's applicability. For example, as of September 2000, the system for processing the state's workers' compensation appeals was essentially halted because the law required parties to obtain the consent of workers to have their medical records examined. Appeal hearings then in process — no matter at what stage — were affected because records that the state possessed and had freely used in proceedings prior to the law's enactment were subject to the medical privacy law. Doctors could not refer to the medical records they had already examined (pre-enactment) in their testimony (post-enactment) without risking criminal prosecution. As a result, the state delayed all cases originally scheduled through March 2001 by 90 days.[252]

The Hawaii Legislature recently created the Access Hawaii Committee,[253] headed by the Governor's Technology Assistant. This committee oversees the State of Hawaii's portal website at www.ehawaiigov.org. The portal will provide the public with interactive government services as well as an electronic method of information distribution. As successful protection of privacy is critical, the committee is developing, in conjunction with the OIP, privacy standards for using the electronic government services program, known as "eHawaii."[254]

[251] *See* Answering Brief of the State of Hawaii at 23-24, *State v. Epps*, Crim. No. 96-1141 (Haw. Nov. 1, 1999).

[252] *See* Daniel B. Moskowitz, *Hawaii Finds Business Hasn't Gotten Ready for Its Comprehensive Medical Privacy Law*, MEDICINE & HEALTH, Sept. 4, 2000, at 2S1.

[253] 2000 Haw. Sess. Laws 292.

[254] Telephone interview with Moya Gray, Director of the Office of Information Practices for the State of Hawaii (Nov. 29, 2000).

KENTUCKY

Kentucky's General Assembly enacted an Open Records Act in 1976.[255] All public records, including those "stored in a computer," must be open for inspection, unless the records are excepted under one of the twelve exemptions to the Act. However, the exemptions are not mandatory, and an agency cannot be penalized for releasing exempted documents.[256] The Act permits agencies to withhold records that contain information of a personal nature, if disclosure would constitute an invasion of privacy; records that are confidentially disclosed to an agency and which are generally recognized as confidential; and recommendations, opinions, and correspondence, as well as preparatory material for such documents, sent to private individuals. The Act also permits the withholding of records the disclosure of which is prohibited by federal law or regulation.[257]

An agency, in its discretion, may make public records available online. It is unlawful to use any public record for a commercial purpose if the requestor did not state such purpose at the time of the request for the record, or if the requestor uses the record for a different commercial purpose than he or she stated.[258]

The disclosure of the following information generally does *not* constitute an invasion of privacy: name, position, and salary of public employee;[259] portions of public employee's resume;[260] and tax delinquencies.[261] The disclosure of the following information generally *does* constitute an invasion of privacy: home address, Social Security number, medical records, marital status;[262] information reflecting that an individual was investigated for a crime for which he or she was not subsequently charged;[263] résumés of

[255] KY. REV. STAT. §§ 61.870 - 61.844

[256] 95-ORD-100 (July 12, 1995); *Board of Edu. v. Lexington-Fayette Urban County Human Rights Comm'n*, 625 S.W.2d 109 (Ky. Ct. App. 1981) (court will balance privacy interest with the interest of the public); *Beckham v. Board of Educ.*, 873 S.W.2d 575 (Ky. 1994) (person who is affected by release of records may contest agency's disclosure).; *Zink v. Commonwealth*, 902 S.W.2d 825, 829 (Ky. Ct. App. 1994) (Social Security number, telephone number, and address constitute clearly unwarranted invasion of personal privacy).

[257] KY. REV. STAT. § 61.878.

[258] *Id.* § 61.874(5), (6).

[259] 98-ORD-184 (Nov. 19, 1998).

[260] OAG 92-59.

[261] 97-ORD-22 (Feb. 5, 1997).

[262] 97-ORD-176 (Nov. 21, 1997).

[263] OAG 91-35.

unsuccessful applicants for public employment;[264] psychological and psychiatric records;[265] credit card numbers;[266] and customer billing records of public utilities.[267] Kentucky has explicitly noted that records protected by the DPPA[268] and by FERPA[269] cannot be released.

Kentucky's Web site promises that it will not provide, rent, or sell personal information to third parties for any purpose, but it may share the information with other state agencies for non-commercial purposes. This guarantee is based on the Kentucky Open Records Act's prohibition on giving out state information for commercial purposes.

In August 1996, a small stir was caused when the Kentucky Department of Education (DOE) accidentally posted personal information of 165 school employees on the Web. The information included names, addresses, bank account numbers, and Social Security numbers. The personal information was part of sample reports posted on the Web to help state employees understand a new state accounting system. The Kentucky DOE said it would thereafter take further measures to protect personal data, including scrambling.[270]

NEW JERSEY

Like the federal constitution, New Jersey's state constitution recognizes and protects a individual's right of privacy from unwarranted governmental intrusion,[271] but like the federal constitution, the New Jersey Constitution contains no broad guarantee of individual privacy such as those provided by the Florida or Hawaii constitutions. The New Jersey Constitution contains a provision identical to the Fourth Amendment to the Unites States Constitution.[272] Under both of these provisions, the people of New Jersey are

[264] OAG 90-113.
[265] OAG 92-10.
[266] 94-ORD-79 (June 27, 1994).
[267] 96-ORD-176 (Aug. 20, 1996).
[268] 98-ORD-1 (Jan. 5, 1998)
[269] OAG 92-177.
[270] *See*, *State to try to Protect Privacy of Teachers on Web*, THE COURIER-JOURNAL OF LOUISVILLE, Aug. 22, 1996, at 2B.
[271] *See* N.J. CONST. art. I, ¶ 7.
[272] *See id.*; U.S. CONST. amend. IV.

assured that they will not be subjected to unreasonable searches and seizures by government agents.[273]

Judicial decisions, however, have allowed individuals to invoke constitutional privacy protection against the government when it seeks to gather or disclose an individual's sensitive personal information.[274] This implied right of privacy in the information-control context is not broad. When individuals invoke the federal or New Jersey constitutions to prevent the state from gathering information or making an unwanted disclosure, the courts weigh the individual's interest in protecting the confidentiality of their personal data against the state's interest in carrying out its regulatory activity.[275]

New Jersey has established a public records law as the foundation of the state's information-management policy.[276] New Jersey's public records law begins with the principle that every citizen of the state has the right to inspect "public records."[277] However, the term "public record" is somewhat narrowly defined as:

> all records *which are required by law to be made, maintained or kept on file* by any board, body, agency, department, commission or official of the State or of any political subdivision thereof or by any public board, body, commission or authority created pursuant to law by the State or any of its political subdivisions, or by any official acting for or on behalf thereof.[278]

Because this definition of a "public record" applies the right to inspect only to those records which are "required by law to be made, maintained or kept on file" there is a realm of state documents that is not subject to public disclosure.[279] Moreover, New Jersey's public records statute allows the executive, legislative and judicial branches to except documents from the

[273] *See* U.S. CONST. amend. IV; N.J. CONST. art. 1, ¶ 7; *In re In-Progress Trace of a Wire Communication*, 386 A.2d 1295, 1298 (N.J. 1978).
[274] *See In re Martin*, 447 A.2d 1290 (N.J. 1982).
[275] *See, e.g.*, *Paul P. v. Verniero*, 170 F.3d 396, 402 (3d Cir. 1999); *Trade Waste Mgmt. Ass'n v. Hughey*, 780 F.2d 221, 234 (3d Cir. 1985); *Doe v. Poritz*, 662 A.2d 367, 407-08 (N.J. 1995).
[276] *See* N.J. STAT. ANN. § 47:1A-1, *et seq.*
[277] *See, e.g.*, *id.* § 47:1A-1 ("The Legislature finds and declares it to be the public policy of this State that public records shall be readily accessible for examination by the citizens of this State, with certain exceptions, for the protection of the public interest.").
[278] *Id.* § 47:1A-2 (emphasis added); *Home News v. Board of Educ.*, 669 A.2d 295 (N.J. Super. Ct. App. Div. 1996).
[279] *See Home News*, 669 A.2d at 297.

scope of the public records statute.[280] This power, which appears to be regularly used, vests certain officials with significant authority to withhold items from public disclosure, enhancing privacy of the state's records at the expense of open government.[281] New Jersey has taken a step-by-step, fine-tuning approach to striking the balance between access and privacy, and the state has opted for a significant degree of privacy in its records.

While the state does not provide an express, general exception to public records disclosure in the context of its "open-records" law, it does so explicitly in the context of closing public meetings where there would be material disclosed "which constitutes an unwarranted invasion of individual privacy such as any records, data, reports, recommendations, or other personal material . . . ."[282] Moreover, numerous individual statutes protect the confidentiality or privacy of specific personal information such as cancer and AIDS data, "'personal and sensitive medical information,'" birth defects, and so on.[283]

It is important to note, however, that New Jersey's tailored statutory open-records scheme is supplemented by a broader common-law right of access to state records.[284] Under New Jersey's common law, a public record is:

> one required by law to be kept, or necessary to be kept in the discharge of a duty imposed by law, or directed by law to serve as a memorial and evidence of something written, said, or done, or a written memorial made by a public officer authorized to perform that function, or a writing filed in a public office. The elements essential to constitute a public record are . . . that it be a written memorial, that it be made by a public officer, and that the officer be authorized by a law to make it.[285]

[280] *See id.*

[281] *See, e.g.*, N.J. STAT. ANN. § 47:1A-2.2 (providing that criminals may not obtain information from the public records regarding their victims unless the information is needed for their defense); *id.* § 9:6-8.11 (providing that state child-abuser reports are not public records).

[282] *Id.* § 10:4-12(b)(3).

[283] *See Home News v. Dep't of Health*, 677 A.2d 195, 197 (N.J. 1996).

[284] *See, e.g.*, *Kuehne Chem. Co., Inc. v. North Jersey Dist. Water Supply Comm'n*, 693 A.2d 168, 171 (N.J. Super. Ct. App. Div. 1997) (noting that New Jersey's common-law right of access is broader than the statutory right).

[285] *Home News v. Board of Educ.*, 669 A.2d at 298 (internal quotation marks omitted, omission in original).

To obtain access to public records under the common law right, "'the applicant must establish that the balance of its interest in disclosure against the public interest in maintaining confidentiality weighs in favor of disclosure.'"[286]

New Jersey's most famous tragedy that relates to access to government information did not stem from a criminal accessing state records to commit an offense. Rather, this tragedy pushed greater public access to government information. In July 1994, seven-year-old Megan Kanka of Hamilton, New Jersey was raped and murdered by a convicted sex offender. Unknown to Megan's parents, the offender resided in Megan's neighborhood.[287] Within months, the New Jersey legislature enacted the first so-called "Megan's Law," which requires convicted sex offenders who are released from prison to register with police departments in the communities in which they live and provides that data to the public.[288]

New Jersey is just beginning the process of evaluating whether the existing record-disclosure system is appropriate for digital records. It is also just beginning the process of moving large amounts of the state's functions and records to an interactive digital format. New Jersey refers to itself as "the online state"[289] and, under the direction of the state's Chief Information Officer, it has recently completed its first "Information Technology Strategic Plan."[290] That plan plays an important part in New Jersey's effort to digitize and make available its electronic records. The plan outlines a number of aggressive steps that the state will be taking over the next three years to increase its electronic government services.[291]

New Jersey is well staffed to handle the ongoing transition to interactive e-government. The state has an Office of Information Technology ("OIT") that provides technical assistance to the state's various agencies in planning and developing the systems necessary to improve the state's digital services.[292] The state also has a CIO who, together with her staff, oversees

[286] *Home News v. Dep't of Health*, 677 A.2d at 198.

[287] *See* Robert D. Butters, *The Implications of "Megan's Law" for Real Estate Practitioners*, THE RISK MGMT. REP., Nov. 1993, *available at* http://www.schinnerer.com/risk_mgmt/real_estate/meganlaw.html.

[288] *See, e.g.*, New Jersey Law Network, Megan's Law, *at* http://www.njlawnet.com/megan.html (last modified July 12, 2000).

[289] See New Jersey's website at http://www.state.nj.us.

[290] *See* OFFICE OF INFO. TECH., STATE OF NEW JERSEY, A GOVERNMENT OF CONNECTIONS: INFORMATION TECHNOLOGY STRATEGIC PLAN (2000), *available at* http://www.state.nj.us/cio/stratplan/stratplan2k.pdf.

[291] *See id.* at ii-iii (CIO's message about the plan).

[292] See OIT's website at http://www.state.nj.us/oit.

the state's information technology initiatives, including serving as the chair of the OIT.[293]

NEW YORK

New York's Freedom of Information Law (FOIL)[294] created the Committee on Open Government (COG) housed in the Department of State. The COG includes a combination of government officials and citizens and it serves as an ombudsman regarding open government issues. The COG is responsible for overseeing and advising with regard to the FOIL, Open Meetings Law (OML),[295] and the Personal Privacy Protection Law (PPPL).[296] The PPPL prohibits the disclosure of personal information without the consent of the data subject, unless an express exception authorizes disclosure. FOIL pertains to the public's right to government records while the OML concerns the public's right to attend meetings of public bodies. The PPPL, enacted in 1984, pertains to personal information collected and maintained by state agencies. State agencies are required to meet a standard of fair information practices regarding the collection, maintenance, use, and disclosure of personal information. The PPPL enables individuals to correct or amend records pertaining to them, it grants individual broad rights of access to records pertaining to them, and it prohibits the release of personal information, except under circumstances specified in the law. "Regulation 1401 Public Access to Records of State and Local Agencies"[297] designates a records access officer and details the responsibilities of that office.

The COG has specific responsibilities under FOIL that involve furnishing advisory opinions, both oral and written, to any person and promulgating rules and regulations relative to procedural aspects of the law. The OML requires that the committee provide advice to any person. Advisory opinions are also prepared concerning the PPPL at the request of persons who are

[293] *See* N.J. Exec. Order No. 87 (Sept. 4, 1998), *available at* http://www.state.nj.us/infobank/circular/eow87.htm.
[294] N.Y. Public Off. Law, art. 6, §§ 84-90, *available at* http://www.dos.state.ny.us/coog/textdocs/art6.txt. For a discussion of this law see http://www.dos.state.ny.us/coog/foil.html.
[295] *Id.* art. 7, §§ 100-111, *available at* http://www.dos.state.ny.us/coog/textdocs/art7.txt. For a discussion of this law see http://www.dos.state.ny.us/coog/oml.html.
[296] *Id.* art. 6A, §§ 91-99, *available at* http://www.dos.state.ny.us/coog/textdocs/pppl.txt. For a discussion of this law see http://www.dos.state.ny.us/coog/pppl.html.
[297] *See id.*

subjects of records covered by the law, as well as at the request of state agencies seeking to comply with that statute.

Additionally the committee is required to submit a single comprehensive annual report to the Governor and the Legislature describing the committee's experiences under each of the statutes and making a recommendation for improving them.[298] Each agency within the body of the New York State Government has a records access officer that is responsible for coordinating that agency's response to a particular request.[299]

Technology Policy Memorandum 97-1 Information Security established Information Security Officers (ISOs) in each agency.[300] Office for Technology Memorandum Policy 99-2 provides the minimum administrative responsibilities for each ISO.[301] The ISO must ensure that information security policies and procedures are established and implemented to protect the information assets of the agency, participate in the creation and review of the policies and procedures, recommend security strategies, and keep information security systems current.[302] The agency must have procedures to prevent, detect, contain and recover from information security breaches.

Additionally, each agency must establish an advisory board representing different functions and disciplines across the organization to help develop policies and procedures and maintain continuity of information security across the agency. All employees, agents, and others who access agency computer systems must be provided with sufficient training and supporting reference materials to allow them to properly protect agency information. Training is an integral aspect of information security and will contribute to a secure computing environment.

TEXAS

Rather than a comprehensive privacy law, Texas has over 580 separate statutes to protect personal privacy. Recently, however, the Legislature

[298] COMM. ON OPEN GOV'T, N.Y. DEP'T OF STATE, 1999 REPORT TO THE GOVERNOR AND THE STATE LEGISLATURE (Dec. 1999), *available at* http://www.dos.state.ny.us/pdfs/co og99rep.pdf.

[299] 21 N.Y. COMP. CODES R. & REGS. tit. 1401, *available at* http://www.dos.state.ny.us/coog/textdocs/reg1401.txt.

[300] Governor's Task Force on Info. Res. Mgmt., Technology Policy 97-1, (Jan. 9, 1997), *available at* http://www.oft.state.ny.us/policy/tp 971.htm.

[301] Office for Tech., Technology Policy 99-2 (Feb. 26, 1999), *available at* http://www.oft.state.ny.us/policy/99-2.htm.

[302] *Id.*

proposed H. J. R. No. 15 as a constitutional amendment relating to a citizen's right of privacy. The proposed amendment would add the following:

> Sec. 8a. The right of every individual to *privacy* is recognized and may not be infringed without the showing of a compelling state interest that may not be achieved in a less intrusive and more reasonable manner.[303]

This proposed constitutional amendment may be submitted to the voters at an election to be held on November 6, 2001.

The Attorney General is responsible for ensuring that Texas government is open and accessible to all citizens. Several divisions of the agency are involved in this effort. The Office of the Attorney General[304] has appointed a Public Information Coordinator (PIC) who is the recipient of all requests for public information held by the Attorney General's office.

The open government statute in Texas is known as the Public Information Act (PIA).[305] It is intended to make State government more transparent and accountable to the people. It is the policy of Texas that each person is entitled, unless otherwise expressly provided by law, to obtain complete information about the affairs of government and the official acts of public officials and employees. Fifteen of the thirty-five exceptions of the PIA deal with the protection of personal information. The information that is protected from disclosure is specific to particular populations and circumstances. For instance, personal information is protected for state employees, crime victims, and prison inmates; specific types of records such as student records and library records are also protected under the exceptions to the PIA. In order for information to be protected under the "common law tort" exception to PIA, it must be of "(1) highly intimate or embarrassing facts about a person's private affairs such that its release would be highly objectionable to a reasonable person and (2) be of no legitimate concern to

[303] H.J.R. No. 15, constitutional amendment for a citizen's right of privacy in Texas, *available at* http://www.capitol.state.tx.us/cgibin/cqcgi?CQ_SESSION_KEY=YOZWHYQKYOWN&CQ_QUERY_HANDLE=123992&CQ_CUR_DOCUMENT=1&CQ_SAVE[bill_number]=HJ00015INT&CQ_TLO_DOC_TEXT=YES (last visited Dec. 19, 2000) (emphasis added).

[304] *See* Office of the Attorney General website, *at* http://www.oag.state.tx.us/agency/agjc_bio.htm (last visited Dec. 18, 2000).

[305] Public Information Act, TEX. GOV'T CODE § 552, *available at* http://www.oag.state.tx.us/AG_Publications/txts/ publicinformation99.rtf (last visited Dec. 19, 2000).

the public."[306] Under the interpretations of the Office of the Attorney General, very little data that is collected by the State is of no legitimate concern to the public. The Attorney General has declared that only express statutory language making information confidential will prevent public record information from being released to the public. The provisions of the Texas PIA are liberally construed to implement a policy of open government.

The Texas Open Government Web site provides a link to its public information handbook to help assist the public in gaining access to public records. The handbook addresses the collection and retention of information by government agencies. The handbook was created to serve as a reference tool for members of the public and special interest groups that inspect public records. The handbook also addresses the options if an agency refuses to produce public records for inspection and copying.

Texas faces four primary data management issues: data collection and retention, assorted and uneven data protections, intergovernmental sharing of information, and data correction.[307] Focusing on the data collection and retention issue, the public has had several pressing concerns such as (1) is every piece of information gathered necessary for providing products or services to the public?; (2) are agency procedures compliant with the PIA?, and (3) how long does data remain with the agency?

The second issue facing Texas is uneven data protections given by different state agencies. In building its new Internet portal "TexasOnline" privacy was a major concern. In fact, the third goal of the State's Strategic Plan for Information Resources Management states that "Texas state government will ensure the privacy, security, and historical integrity of the information and information resources entrusted to government by the people of Texas."[308] There have been suggestions addressing the differences in data protection, the one recurring suggestion is the redaction of data or specific sections of documents. The Texas legislature is considering requiring agencies to ensure that confidential information contained in requested databases and documents be electronically scrambled or redacted.

The third issue facing Texas is intergovernmental sharing of information. This involves the transferring of data between governmental bodies. In order for the public to feel secure in using the TexasOnline portal there must be some uniform standard for privacy protection.

[306] TEXAS OFFICE OF THE ATTORNEY GEN., PUBLIC INFORMATION HANDBOOK (2000).

[307] TEX. DEP'T OF INFO. RES., *supra* note 80, at *Privacy in Texas*. This report was prepared for the EGTF: Strategic Issues Subcommittee.

[308] TEX. DEP'T OF INFO. RES., *Realizing the Vision*, *in* TEXAS CONNECTED SERVICE AT THE SPEED OF LIGHT, STATE STRATEGIC PLAN FOR INFORMATION RESOURCES MANAGEMENT (1999), *available at* http://www.dir.state.tx.us/pubs/99ssp/99ssp.htm.

The fourth issue involves data correction. There have been major concerns about access to and accuracy of information maintained by state agencies. The legislature is currently considering using a single Texas database and maintaining it under rules similar to the federal Fair Credit Reporting Act. This allows citizens access to the information upon request and provides an avenue to challenge incorrect information.

WASHINGTON

The public disclosure law of the State of Washington was passed by citizen initiative in 1972.[309] The public records law is liberally construed while its exemptions from disclosure are narrowly construed in order to promote the public policy in favor of openness. However, Washington recognizes a citizen's right of privacy.[310]

State law exempts certain personal information from public inspection and copying, including the personal information of public school students, public institution patients, and welfare recipients; personal information of employees, appointees, elected officials, or job applicants at any public agency to the extent that disclosure would violate their right to privacy; certain taxpayer information required for assessment or collection of tax; intelligence and investigative records, the identity of crime witnesses and victims, examination data used to administer a license, employment, or academic evaluation; library records which disclose the identity of a library user; personal financial information supplied for export projects or state contract bids; membership lists regulated by the department of licensing; residential addresses and telephone numbers of public utility customers; client records maintained by a domestic violence program or a rape crisis center; and credit card numbers, debit card numbers, electronic check numbers, card expiration dates, or bank or other financial account numbers supplied to an agency for the purpose of electronic transfer of funds.

Thus, Washington state law identifies specific types of information that will not be disclosed because doing so would violate "personal privacy," meaning it would be highly offensive to a reasonable person and be of no legitimate public concern.[311] Every agency must publish a current list of every law that the agency believes exempts or prohibits disclosure of specific

[309] RCW 42.17.251.
[310] RCW 42.17.255.
[311] *Id.* 42.17.310(2) and 42.17.255.

information or records of the agency.[312] Washington's Public Records Act may not be employed to obtain "lists of individuals requested for commercial purposes."[313]

Each state agency is responsible for meeting the state's mandated privacy responsibilities, as well as maintaining its own records and information.[314] A party who has been denied access to a state record may request review by the state attorney general.[315] An agency has the option to inform a person named in a record when the record is subject to a pending record request.[316] A person named in a record may seek to enjoin disclosure of the record.[317] Judicial review of a denial of the opportunity to inspect and copy a requested record may be had in superior court.[318] Even if a record is covered by an exemption from the Public Records Act,[319] the court may nonetheless determine that the exemption is not necessary to protect any privacy right and it may order disclosure of the record.[320] Conversely, the agency may argue that there is a basis for exemption from the disclosure act other than those statutorily provided.[321]

The Digital Mecca of Washington State has produced highly sophisticated Executive Orders, Reports, model principles, as well as a substantial amount of other highly useful and relevant material. Governor Locke issued Executive Order 00-03 regarding Public Records Privacy Protections[322] is a useful model of enlightened executive action that addresses serious public records privacy issues without undermining the values of open government. The Order recognizes that, on the one hand, "as the Internet comes of age, we are experiencing an explosion in the growth of commercial and government electronic databases that contain highly sensitive personal information about individuals," but on the other hand, there are compelling reasons to preserve "open government and the people's right to know. The very existence of our democracy depends on the fundamental principles embodied in our laws

312 RCW 42.17.260(2).
313 *Id.* 42.17.260(9).
314 *Id.* 42.17.320.
315 *Id.* 42.17.325.
316 *Id.* 42.17.330.
317 *Id.*
318 *Id.* 42.17.340(1).
319 *Id.* 42.17.251
320 *Id.* 42.17.310(3).
321 *Cowles Publ'g Co. v. City of Spokane*, 849 P.2d 1271, 1274 (Wash. Ct. App.), *review denied*, 122 Wash. 2d 1013 (1993).
322 Wash. Exec. Order. No. 000-03 (Apr. 25, 2000), *available at* http://www.governor.wa.gov/eo/eo_00-03.htm.

ensuring that we never have secret government. People must be able to trust their government."

Governor Locke notes the existence of a critical distinction between public information and private personal information that happens to be held by the government. Taxpayer information has never been subject to public scrutiny and "citizens [do not] expect that their health records, bank account, or credit card numbers will be open for inspection or available to others."

Governor Locke identified the following principles to enhance the public records privacy protections available in Washington State:

- Minimizing as much as possible the collection, retention, and release of personal information by the state;
- Prohibiting the unauthorized sale of citizens' personal information by state government;
- Providing citizens with broad opportunities to know what personal information about them the state holds, and to review and correct that information; and
- Making certain that businesses that contract with the state use personal information only for the contract purposes and cannot keep or sell the information for other purposes — and that those who violate this trust are held accountable.

The Order defines "personal information" to mean information collected by a state agency about a natural person that is readily identifiable to that specific individual. The Order directs several state government actions, which are reproduced in Appendix C.

In addition to the Executive Order, the Governor established a "Governor's Work Group on Commercial Access to Government Electronic Records."[323] The Group's Final Report provides an excellent summary of the legal and practical issues surrounding the tension between access and privacy

[323] GOVERNOR'S WORK GROUP ON COMMERCIAL ACCESS TO GOV'T ELEC. RECORDS, *Chapter 4: Safeguarding Personal Information, in* IN THE BALANCE: TOWARD A MODEL FOR PUBLIC STEWARDSHIP OF ELECTRONIC GOVERNMENT RECORDS (Final Report 1996), *available at* http://www.wa.gov/dis/commaccess/ch4.htm.

in personal information maintained in public records. Washington has produced several other guides and orders: "Recommended Guidelines for Online Privacy Policy";[324] "Public Records Privacy – Final and Preliminary Reports, State Agency Progress in Implementing Executive Order 00-03";[325] "Overview of EO 00-03 – Public Records Privacy Protections";[326] "Preliminary Agency Results, Privacy Protection Under EO 00-03";[327] a "Model Privacy Notice";[328] and "Designated Agency Privacy Contacts."[329] Washington not only produced the Model Privacy Notice but all executive state agencies and many other agencies have adopted the Notice and have a

[324] State of Wash., Recommended Guidelines for Online Privacy Policy Development (Apr. 26, 2000), *at* http://www.wa.gov/architecture/DISTAAGPrivacy-UsageGuidelines-Draft.htm.

[325] PUBLIC RECORDS PRIVACY – PRELIMINARY REPORT; STATE AGENCY PROGRESS IN IMPLEMENTING EXECUTIVE ORDER 00-03 (Sept. 2000), *at* http://www.governor.wa.gov/recpriv/recprivcont.htm.

[326] *Overview of EO 00-03*, *in* PUBLIC RECORDS PRIVACY – PRELIMINARY REPORT; STATE AGENCY PROGRESS IN IMPLEMENTING EXECUTIVE ORDER 00-03 (Sept. 2000), *at* http://www.governor.wa/gov/recpriv/recpriv.htm.

[327] *Preliminary Agency Results, Privacy Protection Under EO 00-03*, *in* PUBLIC RECORDS PRIVACY – PRELIMINARY REPORT; STATE AGENCY PROGRESS IN IMPLEMENTING EXECUTIVE ORDER 00-03 (Sept. 2000), *at* http://www.governor.wa.gov/recpriv/agencyresults.htm.

[328] *Model Privacy Notice*, *in* PUBLIC RECORDS PRIVACY – PRELIMINARY REPORT; STATE AGENCY PROGRESS IN IMPLEMENTING EXECUTIVE ORDER 00-03 (Sept. 2000), *at* http://www.wa.gov/dis/e-gov/architecture/FinalPrivacyModel.htm.

[329] *Designated Agency Privacy Contacts*, *in* PUBLIC RECORDS PRIVACY – PRELIMINARY REPORT; STATE AGENCY PROGRESS IN IMPLEMENTING EXECUTIVE ORDER 00- 03 (Sept. 2000), *at* http://www.governor.wa.gov/recpriv/contacts.htm.

privacy notice for their Web site and a link from each page where information is collected.

The state legislature has become particularly sensitive to privacy in relation to technology; in March 2000, an unknown entity repeatedly monitored a state senator's use of her state computer, including the senator's e-mails and stock reports.[330]

[330] Dionne Searcey, *Privacy concerns pop up on screen*, THE SEATTLE TIMES, Mar. 25, 2000, at A9.

Appendix B

Washington State Executive Order 00-03 Public Records Privacy Protections

PREAMBLE

WHEREAS, Citizens of the state of Washington are gravely concerned about their privacy, and that concern is well founded. As the Internet comes of age, we are experiencing an explosion in the growth of commercial and government electronic databases that contain highly sensitive personal information about individuals. The businesses and governments that control those databases *must* be responsible. It is state government's added responsibility to protect the personal privacy rights of Washington's citizens and lead the private sector by example and by law.

I am a strong believer in open government and the people's right to know. The very existence of our democracy depends on the fundamental principles embodied in our laws ensuring that we never have secret government. People must be able to trust their government.

There is a critical distinction, however, between public information and private personal information that happens to be held by the government or a business. Simply because certain personal information is in the hands of a third party does not mean that it should be made public or available to anybody willing to pay for it. A taxpayer's sensitive tax information has never been subject to public scrutiny. Nor do citizens expect that their health records, bank account, or credit card numbers will be open for inspection or available to others.

Unfortunately, as citizens, our expectations may exceed the privacy protections provided in law and the practices and policies established by the private sector and public agencies to protect personal information. The information age has created an urgent need for the custodians of data to exercise special care in safeguarding that information.

With this executive order, it is my intent to ensure that state agencies comply fully with state public disclosure and open government laws, while protecting personal information to the maximum extent possible by:

- Placing the government of Washington state at the forefront in protecting the personal information of its citizens;

- Minimizing as much as possible the collection, retention, and release of personal information by the state;

- Prohibiting the unauthorized sale of citizens' personal information by state government;

- Providing citizens with broad opportunities to know what personal information about them the state holds, and to review and correct that information; and

- Making certain that businesses that contract with the state use personal information only for the contract purposes and cannot keep or sell the information for other purposes – and that those who violate this trust are held accountable.

NOW THEREFORE, I, Gary Locke, Governor of the State of Washington, declare my commitment to strengthen privacy protections for personal information held by state agencies, and to the principles of open government and the people's right to know.

WHEREAS, an increasing number of citizens are concerned that personal information held by the state might be used inappropriately, that unauthorized people may have access to it, and that some information may be inaccurate, incomplete, or unnecessary.

WHEREAS, citizens have a right to know how information about them is handled by state agencies and the extent to which that information may be disclosed or kept confidential under the law.

WHEREAS, many state agencies collect, maintain, and dispose of public records that contain highly confidential and sensitive personal information that must be carefully safeguarded. These records contain sensitive and private health, financial, business, or other personally identifiable information. Their inadvertent release, careless storage, or improper disposal could result in embarrassment or harm to individuals and potential liability for the state.

WHEREAS, state agencies have an obligation to protect personal information about citizens, as required by law. They must exercise particular care in protecting records containing sensitive and private health, financial, and other personally identifiable information about individuals, such as Social Security numbers.

WHEREAS, the purpose of this executive order is to direct state agencies, as responsible information custodians, to institute additional privacy protections for personal information and to ensure that people who supply personal information to state agencies know how it will be handled and protected under state law.

I HEREBY ORDER as follows:

For purposes of this executive order, "personal information" means information collected by a state agency about a natural person that is readily identifiable to that specific individual.

1. **Protecting the Confidentiality of Sensitive Personal Information.** Each state agency shall immediately establish procedures and practices for the handling and disposal of public records and copies to provide reasonable assurances that those containing confidential personal information are properly safeguarded.

2. **Protecting Social Security Numbers and other Sensitive Personal Identifiers.** To the extent practicable, each state agency shall eliminate the use of Social Security numbers and other sensitive personal and financial identifying numbers from documents that may be subject to public scrutiny. Each state agency shall also take steps designed reasonably to ensure that appropriate personnel are aware of the new confidentiality requirement under Ch. 56, Laws of 2000, for credit card and debit card numbers, electronic check numbers, card expiration dates, and other financial account numbers connected with the electronic transfer of funds.

3. **Prohibiting the Sale of Personal Information.** Except as otherwise provided by law, state agencies may not sell personal information that they collect from the public or obtain from other public or private entities.

4. **Limitation on Collection and Retention of Personal Information.** State agencies shall limit the collection of personal information to that reasonably necessary for purposes of program implementation, authentication of identity, security, and other legally appropriate agency operations. Agencies shall examine their record retention schedules and retain personal information only as long as needed to carry out the purpose for which it was originally collected, or the minimum period required by law.

5. **Protection of Personal Information used by Contractors.** State agencies that enter into contracts or data sharing agreements with private entities and other governments that involve the use of personal information collected by the agencies shall provide in those contracts that the information may be used solely for the purposes of the contract and shall not be shared with, transferred, or sold to unauthorized third parties. A state agency that receives personal information from another state agency must protect it in the same manner as the original agency that collected the information. Each state agency shall establish reasonable procedures to review, monitor, audit, or investigate the use of personal information by contractors, including, when appropriate, the "salting" of databases to detect unauthorized use, sale, sharing, or transfer of data. Contractual provisions related to breach of the privacy protection of state contracts or agreements shall include, as appropriate, return of all personal information, termination, indemnification of the state, provisions to hold the state harmless, monetary or other sanctions, debarment, or other appropriate ways to maximize protection of citizens' personal information.

6. **Prohibiting the Release of Lists of Individuals for Commercial Purposes.** RCW 42.17.260 prohibits public agencies from giving, selling, or allowing the inspection of lists of individuals, unless specifically authorized or directed by law, if the requester intends to use the information for commercial purposes. The Attorney General in AGO 1998 No. 2 has interpreted "commercial purposes" broadly and has not limited those purposes only to situations in which individuals are contacted for commercial solicitation. For that reason, unless specifically authorized or directed by law, state agencies shall not release lists of individuals if it is known that the requester plans to use the lists for any commercial

purpose, which includes any profit expecting business activity.

7. **Internet Privacy Policies.** Within 30 days of the effective date of this executive order, the Department of Information Services shall, in consultation with other state agencies and affected constituency groups as appropriate, develop a clear and concise model privacy policy for use by state agencies that operate an Internet web site. The privacy policy shall contain at least the following elements: a) the manner in which the personal information is collected; b) the intended uses of the information; c) a brief description of the laws relating to the disclosure and confidentiality of the information with a link to the state public records act and other laws, as appropriate; d) information on the purpose and anticipated effects of the web site's data security practices; e) the consequences of providing or withholding information; f) the agency's procedures for accessing personal information, verifying its accuracy, and making corrections; g) the method by which an individual may make a request or provide notice to the agency concerning the use or misuse of a person's personal information; and h) how the agency may be contacted. Within 60 days of the completion of the model policy, each state agency that operates an Internet web site shall, after consultation with affected constituency groups, adopt the model policy, modified to the minimum extent necessary to address practical and legal considerations specific to that agency. Links to agency privacy policies should be located prominently on each agency's web site home page and on any other page where personal information is collected.

8. **Notification and Correction.** Each state agency that collects personal information shall, to the extent practicable, provide notice to the public at the point of collection that the law may require disclosure of

the information as a public record. Upon request, state agencies shall provide a written statement generally identifying a) the known circumstances under which personal information in public records may be disclosed, and b) the agency's procedures for individuals to review their personal information and recommend corrections to information that they believe to be inaccurate or incomplete. This notice and statement may be included in an agency privacy policy, as specified in item 7 above.

9. **Citizen Complaints and Oversight.** Citizen complaints, questions, or recommendations regarding the implementation of this executive order or the collection and use of personal information by state agencies shall be submitted to the agency that is the custodian or collector of the information. Each agency shall designate a person to handle complaints, questions or recommendations from, and provide information to, the public regarding the collection and use of personal information and the agency's privacy policies. I will designate a person within the Governor's office to monitor and oversee the administration of this executive order and to serve as a point of contact for complaints from the public not addressed by an agency.

10. **Miscellaneous.** Nothing in this executive order shall be construed to prohibit or otherwise impair a lawful investigative or protective activity undertaken by or on behalf of the state. This order does not create any right or benefit, substantive or procedural, at law or in equity, that may be asserted against the state, its officers or employees, or any other person. It prohibits the release of public records only to the extent allowable under law. State agencies shall, in all cases, comply with applicable law. This order is intended only to improve the internal management of the executive branch and enhance compliance with the law. The Governor may grant exceptions to the requirements of this executive order if an agency

can demonstrate that strict compliance results in excessive and unreasonable administrative burdens or interferes with effective administration of the law.

* * *

Appendix C

International Privacy Initiatives

CANADA

Canada's Privacy Act[331] took effect on July 1, 1983, replacing some limited personal information rights set out in Part IV of the Canadian Human Rights Act. According to the preamble to the Act, "These rights were expanded in the Privacy Act to deal with the growing impact of computers on government record keeping." The Act gives Canadians individual control over their personal data in government data banks by providing them a right to examine information about them held by Canada's 110 federal government departments and agencies. Subject to some specific exceptions, individuals may also ask to have any errors corrected and, if the request is refused, require that a notation be attached to the information describing any corrections requested but not made.

"Personal information" includes information relating to the race, national or ethnic origin, color, religion, age, or marital status of the individual; information relating to the education or the medical, criminal, or employment history of the individual; information relating to financial transactions in which the individual has been involved; any identifying number, symbol, or other particular assigned to the individual; the address, fingerprints, or blood type of the individual; the personal opinions or views of the individual, with exceptions; and correspondence sent to a government institution by the individual that is implicitly or explicitly of a private or confidential nature, as well as replies to such correspondence that would reveal the contents of the original correspondence.

The Act applies to information recorded "in any form" and so includes video and audio tape and any electronic format. The Act also establishes a fair information code which requires the federal government to limit its

[331] R.S.C., ch. P-21 (1985) (Can.).

collection of personal information to the minimum needed to operate programs or activities; collect the information, whenever possible, directly from the person concerned; tell the person why the information is being collected and how it will be used; not use the information for other purposes, unless allowed by law; keep the information for long enough to allow the person a reasonable opportunity to obtain access; ensure that the information is as accurate, up-to-date, and complete as possible; and not disclose personal information unless specifically allowed by the Privacy Act or another law.

Under the Privacy Act, a request for access to one's own personal information is to be made in writing to the government institution that has control of the data bank containing the information. Access may be refused only in limited, specified circumstances. An individual may file a complaint with the Privacy Commissioner when the individual believes his or her personal information is not being protected in accordance with the Act or when an individual believes he or she incorrectly has been denied access to information. The Privacy Commissioner is empowered to undertake investigations and report to Parliament. After filing a complaint with the Privacy Commissioner, an individual may file a complaint with a federal court.

The Privacy Act has equal status with the Access to Information Act which allows Canadians to request information within the government's control. However, if information is personal, "privacy protection is paramount over access to information."

In 1992, the Privacy Commissioner published a "Privacy Check List" to provide guidance on how to build privacy into the design and application of new information management systems. In 1994, the Canadian government issued *Blueprint for Renewing Government Services Using Information Technology*, outlining its plan to use advanced computer technology to streamline, re-engineer, and modernize the federal public service. In 1998, the Treasury Board Secretariat published *Policy on the Use of Electronic Networks*,[332] which endorses the Treasury Board's employees' reasonable expectation of privacy in the workplace, even if using government equipment. The policy also limits the circumstances in which senior management can monitor or intercept communications on government networks.

In May 2000, the Canadian government announced that it would dismantle its "big brother" database, which contains data on 33 million Canadians. The earlier revelation of the existence of the database had sparked a nationwide privacy uproar.

[332] *Available at* http://www.tbs-sct.gc.ca/Pubs_pol/ciopubs/TB_CP/uene.html.

AUSTRALIA

Australian privacy law flows from a variety of international sources and Australian statutes. Guidelines issued by the Organization for Economic Cooperation and Development ("OECD") served as an early forerunner to modern Australian privacy rules.[333]

The OECD guidelines address issues that form the foundation for many individual nations' privacy policies (in addition to entities such as the EU): requiring consent, notice of collection and purpose for data use, rights of access to the information, security, and restrictions on transborder flows of data. Another instrument that is a basis for its laws is the International Covenant on Civil and Political Rights, which guarantees, "No one shall be subjected to arbitrary or unlawful interference with his privacy, family, home or correspondence, nor to unlawful attacks on his honor and reputation."[334]

The primary Australian statute dealing with privacy is the Privacy Act of 1988 (Privacy Act). This law articulates general privacy principles for the handling of certain personally identifiable information as well as rules for specific types of information. Known as Australia's "Information Privacy Principles," these standards apply to any government agency and any eligible data held by such an agency. The principles address: the manner and purpose of collection; solicitation of information; storage and security of data; access; accuracy; and limits on disclosure, with exceptions. The principles act as legal prohibitions on the misuse of personal information by agencies: "an agency shall not do an act, or engage in a practice, that breaches an Information Privacy Principle."[335]

The Privacy Act also enacts laws for specific areas of personal information that mostly apply to government agencies but may also cover relevant non-governmental entities. In particular, the law provides protection for (1) personal tax file numbers used by individuals and organizations and (2) information about an individual's credit worthiness held by credit

[333] *See* OECD, *Annex to the Recommendation of the Council of 23 September 1980*; for discussion, see Office of the Privacy Comm'r, Privacy Act & Other Laws, *at* http://www.privacy.gov.au/act/index.html (last visited Jan. 2, 2001). *See also* OECD, Guidelines on the Protection of Privacy and Transborder Flows of Personal Data (Sept. 23, 1980), *available at* http://www.oecd.org/dsti.sti/it/secur/prod/PRIV-EN.htm.

[334] *International Covenant on Civil and Political Rights*, United Nations High Comm'r for Human Rights, art. 17 (1976), *available at* http://www.unhchr.ch/html/menu3/b/a_ccpr.htm.

[335] *See* Privacy Act, pt. III, §§ 14, 16.

reporting agencies and credit providers. The statute requires the OPC to issue guidelines on "the collection, storage, use and security of tax file number information." The rules cover recipients of tax number information, too.[336]

The Privacy Act also established Australia's Office of the Privacy Commissioner (OPC), an independent agency that implements Australian privacy policies and promotes a cultural appreciation for privacy in Australia.[337] The Commissioner is appointed by the Governor-General of Australia to serve a term of seven years.[338] Federal statutes have invested the OPC with a fair amount of influence, ranging from policy areas to privacy dispute adjudication, both in the private and public sectors. Specific functions of the OPC include: information and advice; policy; complaint handling and audits; and education. The OPC mainly covers Australian federal and commonwealth government ministers and departments, credit providers and credit reporting agencies, any organization or individual that handles personal tax file numbers, and any organization or individual handling old, minor criminal conviction information. In addition, the OPC works to promote Australian privacy standards within private corporations and other entities that deal with personal information.[339] In this way, Australia's privacy policy contains a mixture of government-imposed rules and self-regulation.

The OPC provides counsel on privacy matters to individuals and public and private organizations through a Privacy Hotline. The Hotline dispenses general information and advice concerning privacy rights and best practices in privacy standards. In addition, the OPC's Hotline staff helps Australian government agencies and other entities in complying with privacy laws.[340]

The Privacy Act authorizes the OPC to have a policy division that advises on privacy issues proactively or in response to requests from government officials and the private sector. The policy staff may examine legislative proposals and statutes for privacy implications and it is charged broadly to research how technological and social developments effect privacy. When potential damage to privacy protection is discovered, the policy staff researches ways to minimize it.[341]

[336] *Id.* pt. III, §§ 17-18.
[337] *See* Office of the Privacy Comm'r, About the Privacy Commissioner, *at* http://www.privacy.gov.au/about/index.html (last visited Jan. 2, 2001).
[338] Privacy Act of 1988, pt. IV, § 19A (Austl.) (amended 2000),.
[339] *See* Office of the Privacy Comm'r, *supra* note 364.
[340] *See id.*; Privacy Act, pt. IV, § 27(1)(f).
[341] *See id.* pt. IV, § 27(1)(c) and (f).

Complaints and audits are also handled by the OPC. The Privacy Act directs that the OPC may investigate privacy complaints from individuals about acts and practices of government agencies, private organizations, and individuals.[342] However, this jurisdiction is limited. Allowable claims will generally consist of alleged breaches of Australian privacy principles or data-matching, tax, credit-reporting, and health care information laws. By statute, the OPC cannot undertake investigations until after an individual has pursued the complaint with the appropriate government agency or private entity and received an unsatisfactory response.[343] During an investigation, the OPC has evidence-gathering powers over all relevant documents and may conduct hearing-type proceedings complete with witnesses.[344] Most disputes are resolved when respondents agree to take appropriate measures, including a written apology, retraining of staff, changing procedures, or amending or deleting personal information.[345] A small number of matters warrant monetary compensation to redress any loss or damage to an individual.[346]

The Privacy Act also empowers the OPC to audit government agencies and other organizations for their compliance with Australian privacy law and guidelines. The audit power serves as an incentive for compliance and an educational tool to determine whether and how public and non-governmental entities observe privacy protections. The Privacy Act authorizes the OPC to audit compliance with the Information Privacy Principles; examine records of the Commissioner of Taxation with respect to tax file number information and recipients of this information; and audit credit information files and credit reports held by credit reporting agencies and credit providers.[347] Audit reports consist of findings and recommendations, and the Privacy Act allows auditees to respond with either an acceptance or non-acceptance of the findings.

Australia's governmental privacy apparatus performs two functions that are considered unique in international privacy administration. First, almost all governmental bodies at the federal level have a Privacy Contact Officer to serve as the initial point of contact for a privacy complaint prior to pursuing

[342] *See id.* pt. IV, § 27(a) and pt. V; Office of the Privacy Comm'r, What Are My Rights?, *at* http://www.privacy.gov.au/rights/index.html (last visited Jan. 2, 2001).
[343] *See* Privacy Act, pt. V, § 36; Office of the Privacy Comm'r, *supra* note 342.
[344] *See* Privacy Act, pt. V, §§ 44-47. However, the OPC rarely exercises its power to conduct conferences and call witnesses. *See* Office of the Privacy Comm'r, *supra* note 342.
[345] Office of the Privacy Comm'r, *supra* note 342; *see* Privacy Act, pt. V, §§ 52-62.
[346] *Id.*
[347] Privacy Act, pt. IV, §§ 27(1)(h), 28(1)(d)-(e), 28A(1)(g); Office of the Privacy Comm'r, Privacy & the Public Sector, *at* http://www.privacy.gov.au/public/index.html (last visited Jan. 2, 2001).

claims through the OPC.[348] The OPC convenes regular meetings with all Privacy Contact Officers to discuss current privacy issues.[349] Second, the Privacy Act empowers the OPC to make decisions in the public interest.[350] If the OPC determines that an agency's act or practice violates one of the country's Information Privacy Principles, then the OPC may order a halt to the activity. As of January 2001, the OPC has issued six such determinations.[351]

The OPC has issued detailed guidelines for all Australian government Web sites in order to inform agencies of best practices for compliance with the Privacy Act.[352] First, agency Web sites are directed to prominently display Privacy Statements that describe the nature of information collected, its purpose and use, possible disclosure and to whom, and any other relevant issue. This means articulating whether clickstream data or cookies are used and whether or not an e-mail address may be used for future solicitations. Second, in soliciting or collecting information, agencies must adhere to the Information Privacy Principles of the Privacy Act, and must confirm their compliance with them. Third, personal information can only be collected by adequately secure means. Citizens should, if they desire, be allowed to submit their information through an alternative method. Finally, if personal information is published on a Web site or in any other form, the individual must have known about this purpose and given his or her consent.

348 Office of the Privacy Comm'r, *supra* note 347.
349 TEX. DEP'T OF INFO. RES., *supra* note 80, at *Appendix III*.
350 Privacy Act, pt. VI, §§ 71-80.
351 *See* Office of the Privacy Comm'r, *supra* note 347; *see* TEX. DEP'T OF INFO. RES., *supra* note 80, at *Appendix III*.
352 *See* Office of the Privacy Comm'r, Guidelines for Federal and ACT Government World Wide Websites, *at* http://www.privacy.gov.au/issues/p7_2.html (last visited Jan. 2, 2001).

Appendix D

Organizations Working on Electronic Government

There are a variety of organizations working on electronic government. To a greater or lesser degree, all are confronting the privacy issue. The following paragraphs provide a partial sample of a number of ongoing initiatives and relevant activities.

NATIONAL ELECTRONIC COMMERCE COORDINATING COUNCIL (NECCC)

The National Electronic Commerce Coordinating Council (NECCC) is an alliance of national state government associations dedicated to the advancement of electronic government within the states. It is comprised of the National Association of State Information Resource Executives (NASIRE), the National Association of State Purchasing Officials (NASPO), the National Association of State Auditors, Comptrollers and Treasurers (NASACT), and the National Association of Secretaries of State (NASS). The National Governors Association (NGA) and other governmental and private organizations also provide advice and support to the NECCC. The NECCC's goal is to enhance electronic government in the states generally, and digital privacy specifically. The NECCC materials include templates to assist state and local governments in developing and posting Web site privacy policies.

In an impressive array of materials published in December 2000, NECCC addressed a range of electronic government issues. NECCC reviewed the current condition of electronic government by conducting a detailed analysis of over 1,800 state and federal government Web sites, by testing e-mail responses, by studying what kinds of governmental features are available online, and accessing how Web sites respond to citizen requests for information.[353]

Relying on the September 2000 report of Professor Darrell M. West of Brown University, *Assessing e-Government: The Internet, Democracy, and Service Delivery by State and Federal Governments,* NECCC found that "the e-government revolution had fallen short of its potential. Government Web sites are not making full use of available technology, and there are problems in terms of access and democratic outreach. . . . Among the more important findings of the research are . . . only 5% of government Web sites show some form of security policy and 7% have a privacy policy [as of the survey conducted during the summer, 2000]."

A more focused study conducted by NECCC showed that by December 1, 2000, there was a substantial increase in the number of states that had posted privacy policies on their websites. But NECCC observed that:

> Unfortunately, the cities and counties did not show as significant an augmentation in their numbers as the states did. Previously, no city had a privacy policy on their home page. Currently, only San Diego has added one. The largest counties (all with populations over 1.1 million people) did not yield many privacy policy postings either. In March, only Maricopa County, Arizona, had a privacy policy link on their home page. As of December 1, 2000 Maricopa is still the only county to have a privacy policy listed. Policies were absent on the remaining 24 sites.[354]

NATIONAL GOVERNORS ASSOCIATION (NGA)

The National Governors Association (NGA) has established an "NGA e-Governance Task Force" to promote excellence in electronic state government. The NGA has articulated a number of principles for electronic government including: "meeting citizen needs"; "implementing the Internet imperative"; "promoting public trust"; "improving government operations"; and "planning and investing for the future." The NGA Task Force recognizes the latent demand for electronic government, noting that citizens are realizing tremendous benefits through the convenience and richness of

[353] NECCC, Documents Released at the 4th Annual NECCC Conference in Los Vegas, Nevada (Dec. 2000), *available at* http://www.ec3.org.
[354] NECCC, E-Procurement Policy Issues (Dec. 2000), *available at* http://www.ec3.org.

electronic services and transactions in the private sector. "Online shopping, financial services, directories and consumer research, education and entertainment are transforming consumer expectations at a rapid pace. Citizens will expect no less from government."[355]

In addition to the imperative of moving government information on to the Internet, NGA recognizes that citizens expect much more than brochures online. They want to transact their business with government using the Internet. Citizens expect *personalization*.

> As government web applications become more sophisticated, they can use information provided by the citizen/user to personalize the interaction. For example, using zip code information provided by the user, the portal could provide links to the citizen's local government and school system. With additional information and the appropriate security measures, a citizen could get more personalized information from their state web portal, such as copy of their birth certificate or the status of their tax refund.[356]

Of course, in order to maintain and promote public trust, the concern of citizens for the privacy of their personal information must be respected. NGA has recognized that "citizen concerns about privacy are a top priority for the successful deployment of the electronic government."

NATIONAL ASSOCIATION OF ATTORNEYS GENERAL (NAAG)

The National Association of Attorneys General (NAAG) has also gotten involved on Internet issues. NAAG concerns itself primarily with consumer protection issues involving the private sector. NAAG dedicated its summer meeting in June 2000 to privacy. As of December 2000, NAAG had developed draft consumer privacy principles. They were controversial, and have been revised.

[355] www.nga.org/pubs/issuebriefs/2000/electronicgovt.asp.

[356] *Id.*

NATIONAL ACADEMY OF PUBLIC ADMINISTRATORS (NAPA)

The National Academy of Public Administrators (NAPA) is also leading an information practices "clearinghouse" project designed to identify and share privacy-related information. The project will maintain a privacy information clearinghouse comprising a comprehensive collection of information relating to privacy and governmental records. NAPA will also establish a process for identifying emerging privacy issues, convening workshops and conferences and organizing a conference on "Privacy Issues in Electronic Public Records."[357]

OFFICE OF MANAGEMENT AND BUDGET (OMB)

At the federal level, the Office of Management and Budget chairs a Chief Information Officers (CIO) Council established by Executive Order 13011. The CIO Council serves as the principal federal forum for improving federal information technology policy. The CIO Council's website, <cio.gov/egov>, collects a great deal of useful e-Government material.

[357] NAPA, Information Practices Project (IPP) Proposal 1 (Dec. 1, 2000) (unpublished paper on file with author). NAPA's web site is located at http://www.napawash.org.

Selected Resource Materials and Links

Overall Project Resources
http://www.sidley.com/cyberlaw/features/privacydigital.asp

Federal Statutes

FOIA
http://www.usdoj.gov/04foia/foiastat.htm

The Privacy Act of 1974, 5 U.S.C. § 552a
http://www.usdoj.gov/foia/privstat.htm

Electronic FOIA (PL 104-231, 1996)
http://frwebgate.access.gpo.gov/cgi-bin/useftp.cgi?IPaddress=162.140.64.21&filename=publ231.104&directory=/diskc/wais/data/104_cong_public_laws

Internet False Identification Prevention Act of 2000, PL 106-598 (S. 2924 Enrolled Version)
http://thomas.loc.gov/cgi-bin/query/z?c106:S.2924.ENR:

Electronic Freedom of Information Act Amendments of 1996, [[Page 110 Stat. 3048]], Public Law 104-231, 104th Congress
http://www.access.gpo.gov/cgi-bin/getdoc.cgi?dbname=104 cong public_laws

Supreme Court Cases

Olmstead v. US (1928)
http://caselaw.lp.findlaw.com/cgi-bin/getcase.pl?court=us&vol=277&invol=438

Katz v. US (1967)
http://caselaw.lp.findlaw.com/scripts/getcase.pl?navby=search&court=US&case=/us/389/347.html

Whalen v. Roe (1975)
http://caselaw.lp.findlaw.com/scripts/getcase.pl?navby=search&court=US&case=/us/423/1313.html

Richmond Newspapers, Inc. v. Virginia (1980)
http://caselaw.lp.findlaw.com/scripts/getcase.pl?navby=search&court=US&case=/us/448/555.html

Press-Enterprise Co. v. Superior Court (1984)
http://caselaw.lp.findlaw.com/cgi-bin/getcase.pl?navby=case&court=us&vol=464&invol=501#510

Press-Enterprise Co. v. Superior Court (1986)
http://caselaw.lp.findlaw.com/scripts/getcase.pl?navby=search&court=US&case=/us/478/1.html

DOJ v. Reporters Committee (1989)
http://caselaw.lp.findlaw.com/scripts/getcase.pl?navby=search&court=US&case=/us/489/749.html

LA Police Dept v. United Reporting Publishing Corp. (1999)
http://caselaw.lp.findlaw.com/scripts/getcase.pl?court=us&vol=000&invol=98-678

Reno v. Condon (2000)
http://caselaw.lp.findlaw.com/scripts/getcase.pl?court=us&vol=000&invol=98-1464

Bartnicki v. Vopper (2001)
http://caselaw.lp.findlaw.com/scripts/getcase.pl?navby=search&court=US&case=/us/000/99%2D1687.html

Kyllo v. U.S. (2001)
http://caselaw.lp.findlaw.com/scripts/getcase.pl?navby=search&court=US&case=/us/000/99%2D8508.html

Federal Executive Materials

Memorandum for the Heads of Executive Departments and Agencies
FROM: Jacob J. Lew, Director
SUBJECT: Privacy Policies and Data Collection on Federal Web Sites
http://www.whitehouse.gov/OMB/memoranda/m00-13.html

Memorandum for the Heads of Executive Agencies
FROM: Franklin D. Raines, Director
SUBJECT: Guidance on Developing a Handbook for Individuals Seeking Access to Public Information
http://www.whitehouse.gov/OMB/memoranda/m97-10.html

Statement of Hon. Joshua Gotbaum, Acting Deputy Director for Management, U.S. Office of Management and Budget, before the Subcommittee on management, Information, and Technology Committee on Government Reform and Oversight, U.S. House of Representatives, June 14, 2000
http://www.whitehouse.gov/OMB/legislative/testimony/June_14_2000.html

Memorandum for Heads of Departments and Agencies
FROM: Jacob J. Lew
SUBJECT: Instructions on complying with President's Memorandum of May 14, 1998, "Privacy and Personal Information in Federal Records"
http://www.whitehouse.gov/OMB/memoranda/m99-05.html

The White House, Washington, May 14, 1998, Memorandum for the Heads of Executive Departments and Agencies
SUBJECT: Privacy and Personal Information in Federal Records
http://www.whitehouse.gov/OMB/memoranda/m99-05-a.html

Instructions for Complying with the President's Memorandum of May 14, 1998, "Privacy and Personal Information in Federal Records"
http://www.whitehouse.gov/OMB/memoranda/m99-05-b.html

Governmentwide Systems of Records
http://www.whitehouse.gov/OMB/memoranda/m99-05-c.html

Memorandum for Agency Chief Information Officers
FROM: Donald Arbuckle
SUBJECT: Biennial Privacy Act and Computer Matching Reports
http://www.whitehouse.gov/OMB/inforeg/datacall.html

Memorandum for the Heads of Executive Departments and Agencies
FROM: Jacob J. Lew, Director
SUBJECT: Privacy Policies on Federal Web Sites
http://www.whitehouse.gov/OMB/memoranda/m99-18.html

June 1, 1999, Guidance and Model Language for Federal Web Site Privacy Policies
http://www.whitehouse.gov/OMB/memoranda/m99-18attach.html

May 19, 1998, Memorandum for the Chief Information Officers Council
FROM: G. Edward DeSeve, Acting Deputy Director for Management
SUBJECT: Instructions for Reporting Status of Data Exchanges with the States
http://www.whitehouse.gov/OMB/inforeg/dataex.html

Memorandum for the Heads of Executive Agencies
FROM: Franklin D. Raines
SUBJECT: Updated Guidance on Developing a Handbook for Individuals Seeking Access to Public Information
http://www.whitehouse.gov/OMB/memoranda/m9809.html

OMB Bulletin No. 95-01, To the Heads of Executive Departments and Establishments
SUBJECT: Establishment of Government Information Locator Service
http://www.whitehouse.gov/OMB/bulletins/95-01.html

M-97-10, Memorandum for the Heads of Executive Agencies
FROM: Franklin D. Raines, Director
SUBJECT: Guidance on Developing a Handbook for Individuals Seeking Access to Public Information

http://www.whitehouse.gov/OMB/memoranda/m97-10.html

Circular No. A-130, Revised, (Transmittal Memorandum No. 3), (Accompanying Federal Register Materials – Feb. 1996), Memorandum for Heads of Executive Departments and Establishments
SUBJECT: Management of Federal Information Resources
http://www.whitehouse.gov/OMB/circulars/a130/a130.html

United States of America, Federal Trade Commission, Washington, D.C. 20580, September 22, 2000, Comments on Study of Privacy Issues in Bankruptcy Data
http://www.ftc.gov/be/v000013.htm

December 15, 1999, Privacy and Access to Electronic Case Files in the Federal Courts
http://www.uscourts.gov/privacyn.htm

A Citizens Guide on Using the Freedom of Information Act and the Privacy Act of 1974 to Request Government Records
http://www.house.gov/reform/reports/foia.htm

Request for Comment on Privacy and Public Access to Electronic Case Files
http://www.privacy.uscourts.gov/RFC.htm

State Materials

Hawaii

State Constitution, The Constitution of the State of Hawaii
http://www.hawaii.gov/lrb/con/conart1.html

The Commercial Use of Personal Information, December 1999, Office of Information Practices, State of Hawaii
http://www.hawaii.gov/oip/privacy_report_1999.htm

California

California Constitution, Article 1 Declaration of Rights
http://www.leginfo.ca.gov/cgi-bin/waisgate?waisdocid=7365327096+0+0+0&waisaction=retrieve

Washington

State of Washington, Recommended Guidelines for Online Privacy Policy Development, April 26, 2000
http://www.wa.gov/dis/e-gov/architecture/DISTAAGPrivacy-UsageGuidelines-Draft7.htm

Washington State, Governor's Work Group on Commercial Access to Government Electronic Records, Final Report, Chapter 4: Safeguarding Personal Information
http://www.wa.gov/dis/commaccess/ch4.htm

Washington State, Executive Order 00-03, Public Records Privacy Protections
http://www.governor.wa.gov/eo/eo_00-03.htm

Public Records Privacy – Final Report, State Agency Progress in Implementing Executive Order 00-03, November 2000
http://www.governor.wa.gov/recpriv/recprivcont2.htm

Primary Agency Results, Privacy Protection Under EO 00-03 (as of July 2000)
http://www.governor.wa.gov/recpriv/agencyresults.htm

Recommended Guidelines for Online Privacy Policy Development
http://www.wa.gov/dis/e-gov/architecture/usage.htm

Model Privacy Notice
http://www.wa.gov/dis/e-gov/architecture/FinalPrivacyModel.htm

Designated Agency Privacy Contacts, Executive Cabinet
http://www.governor.wa.gov/recpriv/contacts.htm

Consumer Privacy Workgroup, Report to the Attorney General, January 10, 2000
http://www.wa.gov/ago/privacy/Privacy_report.html

Texas
Privacy Issues Involved in Electronic Government, Prepared for the Electronic Government Task Force: Strategic Issues Subcommittee By the Department of Information Resources, August 2000, Austin, Texas
http://www.dir.state.tx.us/egov/report/privacy.html

Privacy Acts of the States and the United States
http://www.oag.state.tx.us/notice/privacy_table.htm

Information Held by Governmental Bodies Deemed Private or Confidential by the Texas Constitution and Statutes, Compiled by The Office of the Attorney General of Texas at the Request of The House Committee on State Affairs, Subcommittee on Privacy Issues, July 20, 2000, Information Held by Governmental Bodies Deemed Private or Confidential by the Texas Constitution and Statutes
http://www.oag.state.tx.us/notice/privacy_statutes.htm

Academic and NGO Materials

The Public Record: Information Privacy and Access, A New Framework for Finding the Balance, by Fred H. Cate and Richard J. Varn
http://www.cspra.org

Assessing E-Government: The Internet, Democracy, and Service Delivery by State and Federal Governments, by Darrell M. West, Brown University, Providence, RI 029912
http://www.insidepolitics.org/egovtreport00.html

Privacy As Censorship: A Skeptical View of Proposals to Regulate Privacy in the Private Sector, by Solveig Singleton
http://www.cato.org/pubs/pas/pa-295.html

National Academy of Public Administration, Information Practices Project (IPP) Proposal
http://www.napawash.org

NECCC E-Procurement Policy Issues Version III, NECCC December, 2000
http://www.ec3.org

NECCC Risk Assessment Guidebook for e-Commerce/e-Government, NECCC December, 2000
http://www.ec3.org

Lost and Found in Cyberspace: Informational Privacy in the Age of the Internet, Susan E. Gindin
http://www.info-law.com/lost.html

Privacy – Building the Public Trust, Information Technology Task Force, National Governors' Association Center for Best Practices
http://www.nga.org/center/divisions/1,1188,C_ISSUE_BRIEF^D_388,00.html

From Cradle to Grave: Government Records and Your Privacy, Privacy Rights Clearinghouse
http://www.privacyrights.org/fs/fs11-pub.htm

Public Records: Access, Privacy, and Public Policy, A Discussion Paper Prepared by Robert Gellman, Consultation on Public Records April 21, 1995; © 1995 All Rights Reserved. Revised Draft May 16, 1995
http://www.cdt.org/privacy/pubrecs/pubrec.html

Privacy Policies – Are you Prepared – A Guide for State and Local Government (Version III), December 2000
http://www.ec3.org

Real Estate Solutions: The Value of Open Public Record
http://www.firstamres.com/html/11_OpenPublicRecord.html

Electronic Privacy Information Center, Legislative Survey of State Confidentiality Laws, with Specific Emphasis on HIV and Immunization
http://www.epic.org/privacy/medical/cdc_survey.html

International Materials

Australia

Privacy in Australia, Office of the Federal Privacy Commissioner
http://www.privacy.gov.au

United Kingdom

Government Policy on Archives, Presented to Parliament by the Lord High Chancellor by Command of Her Majesty, December 1999, Lord Chancellor's Department, Selborne House, 54-60, Victoria Street, London,SW1E 6Qw, Tel. 020 7210 8500
http://www.pro.gov.uk/archives/archivepolicy/fullpolicy.htm

About the Author

ALAN CHARLES RAUL is a partner in the Washington, D.C. office of the international law firm of Sidley Austin Brown & Wood. Mr. Raul has broad experience in the areas of administrative and constitutional law. He concentrates on issues involving science, technology and law, including Internet and E-Commerce law, intellectual property, privacy, and environment, health and safety issues. His practice involves general and appellate litigation, and business counseling.

Mr. Raul has participated in a number of high profile "law and science" cases involving judicial review of federal regulations. He represents clients in cases involving the Lanham and Trademark Acts, the Digital Millennium Copyright Act, the Electronic Communications Privacy Act, and the Anticybersquatting Consumer Protection Act, as well as arbitration proceedings conducted by the World Intellectual Property Organization (WIPO) regarding Internet domain names. He also represents clients on various public policy and regulatory issues, and international trade matters.

Mr. Raul coordinates the Firm's CyberLaw practice in Washington and the Firm's Internet Law web site at www.sidley.com/cyberlaw. He serves as Senior Fellow of the Progress and Freedom Foundation. He serves as a member of the Advisory Council for the Atlantic Legal Foundation, and has also served on the Membership Implementation Task Force of the Internet Corporation for Assigned Names and Numbers (ICANN). Mr. Raul speaks frequently on Internet topics, "junk science," and federal regulatory policy. He has published numerous articles in legal periodicals, as well as in The Wall Street Journal, Washington Post, Los Angeles Times, and eCompany Now. He also appears frequently as a legal commentator on various television and radio networks, and testifies before Congress on various issues.

Mr. Raul served as General Counsel of the U.S. Department of Agriculture (1989-1993), and as General Counsel of the Office of Management and Budget in the Executive Office of the President (1988-1989). Before that, he served in the White House as Associate Counsel to the President (1986-1988). During his tenure as Associate Counsel to the

President, Mr. Raul represented the White House in connection with the Iran-Contra investigations.

Mr. Raul graduated from Harvard College (A.B. 1975), Harvard University's Kennedy School of Government (M.P.A. 1977), and Yale Law School (J.D. 1980). Mr. Raul clerked for Judge Malcolm R. Wilkey of the U.S. Court of Appeals for the District of Columbia Circuit. He is a member of the Council on Foreign Relations, and has served in various leadership positions in the Federalist Society, the American Bar Association and the American Heart Association. He lives in Washington, D.C., with his wife, Mary, and three children.

Index